AND THE RIVER STILL SINGS

And the River Still Sings

A WILDERNESS DWELLER'S JOURNEY

Chris Czajkowski

To Jackie
Live out your Dream
Chris Czajkowski

CAITLIN PRESS
Halfmoon Bay, BC

Caitlin Press Inc.
8100 Alderwood Road,
Halfmoon Bay, BC V0N 1Y1
caitlin-press.com

Text design by Kathleen Fraser.
Cover design by Vici Johnstone.
Cover image copyright Patrice Halley Photography.
Printed in Canada on FSC-certified paper using 100 percent post-consumer
waste. The paper is acid- and chlorine-free and is ancient-forest friendly.

Caitlin Press Inc. acknowledges financial support from the Government of
Canada through the Canada Book Fund and the Canada Council for the Arts,
and from the Province of British Columbia through the British Columbia Arts
Council and the Book Publisher's Tax Credit.

Conseil des arts   Canada Council
du Canada   for the Arts

BRITISH COLUMBIA
ARTS COUNCIL
An agency of the Province of British Columbia

Library and Archives Canada Cataloguing in Publication

Czajkowski, Chris, author
       And the river still sings : a wilderness dweller's journey / Chris
Czajkowski.

ISBN 978-1-927575-50-5 (pbk.)

       1. Czajkowski, Chris. 2. Outdoor life—British Columbia—Chilcotin
Ranges. 3. Wilderness survival—British Columbia—Chilcotin Ranges.
4. Solitude—British Columbia—Chilcotin Ranges. 5. Women travellers—
Great Britain—Biography. I. Title.

GV191.52.C93A3 2014   796.5092   C2014-904079-2

*Once upon a time there was a queen living in the land
of the morning sun and the crooked woods. It was a big
and beautiful queendom and there were a lot of contented subjects living in it. First there were the flowers.
They had a big gathering every year in the meadows
below the treeline and the queen walked all the way to
the meadows to join the gathering. The flowers know
that she will be coming and so they put [on] their most
beautiful colours to impress the queen ...*

*One day a musician travelled through the queendom
and stayed for a few days. The queen showed him the
way through the mountains behind the palace ... and
he had some of the most beautiful days in his life ... He
promised to come back and see her again.*

— Janis Bikos,
written in the
guest book at
Nuk Tessli

*All experience is an arch wherethrough
Gleams that untravelled world whose margin fades
Forever and forever when I move*
— Tennyson, "Ulysses"

Contents

Introduction

I sit by my window and wait for a plane. This is something I have done many times during the last thirty years. The plane might already be threading the air between the mountains from the float plane base forty-five kilometres north, but I have no means of finding out for sure. I am not by nature a patient person, but indeterminate waits for light aircraft have been an integral part of my life for more than half of it, and I am by no means young. Most people prefer to fly in this country. There are no roads: the only other way to get here is to carry a camp on your back, and walk.

It is a beautiful, late June morning. The ice went out about three weeks ago; the lake is blue and sparkling, and the low mountains that lift beyond the far shore are still thickly brushed with snow. Behind me, out of sight from where I sit, much bigger peaks sprawl across the horizon. They are bound with the chains of winter, and they will stay wrinkled with glaciers even at the end of a hot, dry summer; now, the winter snow lies heavily upon them. It is from these mountains that the wind comes: the west wind that is called *nuk tessli* in the Carrier language. It can scream like a banshee and pound like a demon, forcing me to fit my life around it. When the winter blizzards boom and roar I shrink within the cabin walls and wait for them to end. I called the small resort I have created here in honour of it: Nuk Tessli. I can never forget the wind's power. But when blackflies hover in a swarm around my head, or a float plane needs to take off with a maximum load on a hot day, *nuk tessli* is a friend. The breeze that comes from the mountains this morning is perfect for flying; it does no more than fracture the sunlight on the lake into sparkling shards.

Nuk Tessli, the resort, comprises three cabins: two I built alone, and the last one with some help. They cluster loosely on a squarish point of land jutting into a lake only three hundred metres below the treeline. There are no other buildings for many kilometres in any direction and certainly nothing else on the lake; the nearest man-made structure is a day's walk away, an outlying cabin belonging to a resort near the float plane base. It is occupied only during the height of the short tourist season, and has never been used as a home.

The scrubby upper montane forest that surrounds Nuk Tessli is much battered by the elements and distorted by mistletoe and other diseases. Some of the trees are lodgepole pines, a species that is universal to most of western Canada, but about half are whitebark pines (a very different tree to the eastern white pine). Whitebarks grow only at high altitudes. When I first came here, I did not know this tree existed, but was puzzled by artifacts that I occasionally found on the aromatic duff between the boulders on the forest floor: cones that looked like a corn cob stripped of its grain, and shells of what appeared to be a small nut. Few people had travelled this country on foot, and even fewer could distinguish this tree, but I eventually learned that this pine had a cone resembling a resin-encrusted hand-grenade. It enclosed wingless pine nuts. The nuts never fall out of their container and cannot be spread by wind, but the tiny capsules are rich in oil and much sought after by squirrels, birds and even grizzly bears. The Clark's nutcracker, a small black, grey and white crow that is common in the area, has a symbiotic relationship with this tree. It caches seeds in open spaces and never eats them all, thus repopulating forests after a burn. The whitebark's timber has a pretty pinkish cast to it, but it makes a soft, weak lumber that splits easily, so I used lodgepole for the main structures of the cabins and whitebark for wall fillers and floorboards.

When I first stood on this point a quarter of a century ago, I had eyes only for the spectacular view. It was August and the weather was brilliant. I thought nothing of the problems that might arise trying to establish myself in such a remote and difficult spot. I had already built one cabin in the wilderness and I expected challenges, but failure did not enter my mind. Two years later on a dull day in early July, when I came to start building and really looked at the place, the awful logistics of manoeuvring logs single-handedly over the tumbled pile of boulders made me wonder if I was crazy. I almost gave up right then. But I made the first chainsaw cut, felled the first tree, and Nuk Tessli was born.

The de Havilland Beaver I am expecting today will come from Nimpo Lake. The forty-five-kilometre flight will take twenty minutes, a far cry from the overland journey, which may require as much as four days in winter. I have occasionally managed it in a fourteen-hour summer hike made in a single day, but conditions could never be guaranteed and I always carried a camp.

Nimpo Lake (named after a dead horse, apparently, but no one can tell me why the horse was called that) is a blink of an eye on the lonely ribbon of Highway 20 that runs west from Williams Lake to Bella Coola. It is about five hundred kilometres north of Vancouver, British Columbia, but the road to Nimpo doglegs to avoid the mountains, and the drive takes nine or ten hours. Downtown Nimpo comprises three buildings: a store; a post office, which is a little cubby hole in a building that does duty as both a Christian school and a restaurant during the week; and a bakery and garage combined. Some years, as many as three float plane companies have operated from the waterfront; now there is only one. Half a dozen resorts are spread around the lake. Winter population is probably around eighty; there may be three times as many in summer. Williams Lake, the nearest town large enough to have a bank, traffic lights, and supermarkets, is four hours' drive east. All supplies and most visitors must travel over that long highway one way or another, although some people elect to use the sixteen-passenger, three-times-a-week scheduled flight from Vancouver to Anahim Lake, from where they are then driven to Nimpo. No matter how they reach the float plane base, however, all complete the journey to Nuk Tessli in that overgrown mosquito as it buzzes and bumps its way through the mountains.

I have never liked flying and, until recent years, always made the journey on foot. The hike is not an easy one: there is no designated path. Abandoned trappers' trails that once carved a route through the forested sections have long since grown over, and the ten-kilometre stretch of alpine tundra has never been marked. No problem in good weather, but whiteouts and blizzards can occur even in summer up there. In early winter it is best to stay buried in the forest and follow the river down; it is a miserable trip through swamps and a multitude of windfalls, but safer than going above the treeline at that time of year. In late winter, when the high-altitude snow is hard and the days are long, it is possible to make much better time in the alpine, especially when a bright moon can extend the hours during which one can travel. On one memorable occasion in winter, when I was diverted by a blizzard, the trip took six days—and I had food for only three. I and my two pack dogs were a tad hungry at the end of it.

A variety of small planes are used by private pilots who sometimes come and go, but the commercial companies generally prefer two kinds. The smaller is the Cessna 185. It holds three passengers or three hundred kilograms of freight when taking off at Nimpo on floats, and needs a long runway to get airborne. The de Havilland Beaver carries six seats and can lift off in a much shorter distance with 550 kilograms of freight. Neither plane can carry as much when leaving Nuk Tessli due to the lake's smaller size and higher altitude. Occasionally, in hot, still weather, the Cessna might not make it. The pilot must either wait for cooler temperatures or a wind, or fly part of his cargo in one trip and come back for the rest.

Today, conditions are perfect up here; the sky is clear, the air is cool and stable, the breeze is designed for maximum lift. I do not know exactly when the plane will arrive, however. "The last half of the morning," the man I am waiting for informed me by satellite Internet yesterday evening. I cannot get more up-to-date information. My radiophone operates through a private frequency that the float plane company is not a party to, and I use it for emergencies only—besides, it does not work half the time. And whereas the satellite Internet gives me reliable communication with the outside, the float plane company is a dinosaur in these matters and they may not check their messages for days. This lack of communication is nothing unusual. Before I had the Internet, planes would come here without any warning at all. During inclement weather, people might arrive a day late. When I first came here I had no means of contacting anyone whatsoever. Not even a radiophone. My only communication with the outside world was a monthly mail trip, which I completed on foot. The only safety backup was the hope that, if I were ever overdue, someone would come looking for me. I had supreme faith in my survival.

The visitor who is arriving today emailed me from Williams Lake. He planned to spend the night there. He had some business to do before he left, and then would have the four-hour drive to Nimpo. He is not a local man and does not know his way round Williams Lake very well, so who knows how long his chores will take? I rather think "late morning" is wishful thinking on his behalf; still, I must be ready for him. Even if he arrives when he hopes to, the float plane company can never guarantee its schedule. Times for loading and unloading freight and passengers vary, and there are always odd little problems to deal with. Sometimes it is foggy down at Nimpo when it is beautifully sunny at Nuk Tessli. There is no structure in place in this country for instrument flying: if the pilot cannot see, the plane cannot fly. I have never once, in all my time here, received voluntary explanations for delays. If a plane is two hours overdue, I will try to contact the float plane base; I may or may not receive a reply before the pilot arrives.

And so I watch the sun creep across the sky and dance over the little wavelets on the water. The dishes are done, the cabin is tidy, yesterday's fresh-baked bread sits on the counter: all part of the usual welcome package for a guest. There are chores I could be doing, but I have clean clothes on and most work around Nuk Tessli is dirty. Besides, I am restless and cannot settle to anything. The wood stove ticks as it keeps the kettle warm and there is nothing for me to do but sit by the window and wait, as I have done so many times before.

Only this time, it is different.

Birth of an Explorer

Maps, for me, are dreamscapes. I've always been good both at reading them, and at reading the landscape into them. When we were children, my brother was given a *Times World Atlas* published in the late eighteen hundreds. It was a large volume covered in worn leather with slightly faded gold writing recessed into the front. Presumably the European countries were entered fully—I don't remember being particularly interested in them—but the maps of places like Australia and Africa fired my imagination. A thin sepia band around the coasts was marked in great detail, bristling with elegant copperplate script naming every point and inlet and embryonic settlement. The interiors of these continents were white, and a single pale grey word described them: "Unexplored."

My brother and I were raised at the edge of the Fens in Lincolnshire, which is in the East Midlands of England. The Fens are a county-sized tract of land that was originally brackish marsh. About four hundred years ago, Queen Elizabeth I hired the Dutch to drain it; dikes, windmills and houses with Dutch gable ends are a legacy of their time in the area. Part of the Fens is even called Holland. The draining process produced very fertile farmland. Potatoes, grain, sugar beets and tulips were the main crops when I was growing up. Unlike in most of the rest of the country, fields were not divided by walls or hedgerows, only ditches and canals. It was a land of open skies. It was also dead flat.

I was eight years old the first time I experienced a landscape that went up and down. For my birthday I was taken on a railway day excursion to the Peak District. I was instantly hooked. I didn't analyze my feelings then, of course, but I was inexplicably excited by the naked diagonals and sense of space. On the journey home, every time the train passed through a gully and the land viewed through the window sloped to the sky, my heart soared with it. Who knows why this should be? I was brought up in gentle, rural, very level conditions, unaware of any hardship despite what must have been a very difficult time for my parents, so what was it that drew me to this tilted emptiness?

My father was a Polish refugee in the Second World War, and my mother was English-born. My Polish grandfather was a builder. I didn't find this out until recently, long after I had created structures of my own. Before the First World War, Grandfather owned sawmills and the rights to forests beside the Vistula River; his employees would build rafts of the logs and camp on them for a couple of days, Huckleberry Finn–style, while they floated them down to the mill. Grandfather got the contract to build the first railway stations across Poland—all five of them! He also constructed a good part of the village my dad grew up in. I've seen pictures of it: wood is not a predominant feature of these buildings. Most are made of brick.

Both my parents' lives were severely compromised by the war. For six years they had absolutely no choice in what they were able to do. They married when it ended; my brother was born first and I followed soon afterwards. Dad was an independent soul who would never have been happy working for someone else. Although neither parent had much money, they bought a sprawling brick structure that had once been a laundry at the edge of a large village.

Mum would certainly have preferred something farther south: she came from Berkshire and, like all southerners, considered

The old laundry, my childhood home.

anything north of London to be uncouth. No doubt lack of finances didn't give them much choice of location, particularly as they wanted a place with specific requirements. It would have to be suitable for a business as well as a home. The old laundry had three large rooms at one end (one still contained a cistern pump taller than I was, and the remnants of huge mangles) and what had been offices at the other. The offices had already been crudely converted to living quarters. Dad used the laundry part for a shop where he built furniture and restored antiques. This is a full-time occupation in Europe, not a hobby industry as so often happens over here. Much of my childhood was spent playing with long, curly shavings produced by my dad's bench planer and constructing things with his tools. My mother was also very good with her hands, and slowly my parents made the house their own. If things were bought, they were old and my parents refurbished them. Many items were made from scratch. So probably the first useful lesson I learned was if you want something, you make it.

Exactly why I was a loner, I cannot be sure. That my parents did not mix socially might have been one reason, although my

My family. I am sitting with my customary elegance.

brother was gregarious enough. Neighbours were scattered along the quiet village road, but there were very few kids; besides, they were not only younger than I was, but also of a different *class*. Even if I had shown an inclination to do so, I was not encouraged to associate with them. This sounds horrible now, but I was not aware of the British class system until I left. It was nothing to do with income: we probably had less than the neighbours. Unlike them, we had no television, washing machine, fridge or car. Travel, except for a couple of trips a year by train, was by bicycle. Mine was second-hand of course, but fairly modern for the time—it had three gears. Nonetheless it was often hard work getting anywhere because the flatness of the country was no barrier to the wind.

Because we were at the edge of the village, behind our road were woods and fields, and beyond those a chunk of planted forest surrounding an old aerodrome that had been established during the war. I can remember being taken for bike rides as a very small child along the perimeter road of this airfield, which was still being used to store row after row of massive bombs—barrel-sized eggs with points. Rabbits ran through the forestry fence and played hide and seek among the arsenal. The bombs soon disappeared. I wonder how they were disposed of.

. . . .

It wasn't long before I was exploring on my own. I became a prodigious walker. Mum fed birds in the garden and showed me nests in the hedges, and once a week, at lunch time, we listened to a naturalist program on the radio. But why I became so fascinated with nature I am not sure. It was the only thing I was really interested in apart from reading. I walked alone through the countryside, hopping over boundary fences to private lands with impunity and often ignoring established paths. I knew where many local creatures lived, even the snakes, and was always delighted to observe some new animal behaviour. British naturalists include all creatures in their repertoire, be they small mammals, reptiles, birds or insects. This is very different from North America, where "wildlife" generally means something you can shoot. I could also identify all the local wildflowers, but have no recollection of attempting to learn them. I seemed to have absorbed this knowledge by osmosis.

I was channelled into an academic school (by virtue of the now-defunct 11-plus exam) and studied Latin as well as the usual subjects. There was no choice: we had to learn everything on the curriculum. I had a very minimal introduction to art, and only one year of domestic science. From the age of eleven on, I was groomed for university. I was, however, an average student. I was way ahead of the class in subjects that I was interested in, but lazy with anything that required work. For some reason, the biology master never gave me good marks even though I knew so much about the natural world. It was probably because, although I tried, I didn't set the data out in the required fashion. English composition was the subject that gave me my best marks. I used to be perfect in spelling until I started learning French—now my editors return drafts of my manuscripts with red corrections on every line.

On the whole I didn't like school. I was bored and hated being confined to a classroom, particularly in summer; the only way I could tolerate it then was to go for a hike before breakfast. The dawn chorus in those days was a roar of birdsong, but my best memory of these wonderful morning walks is listening to the legendary nightingales. My mother was angry with me for doing this as she felt I should sleep later or my schoolwork would suffer, but I have always been a morning person and would defy her constantly. Problem was I would have to sneak past my parents' open bedroom door and get down the stairs without treading on the ones that creaked.

My final exam results were moderate. I didn't work very hard for them because I had no idea what I wanted to do with my life. I was never interested in cities, pubs, dancing or standard careers, and had no particular friends. I once vowed that I would never live in a town or city and my mother smiled at that, but in fact I never have. I would have liked to be an animal collector like Gerald Durrell or David Attenborough, whose books I devoured. But Mum told me that you needed either lots of money or a very good education for that kind of thing and she was quick to point out that I had neither. Because I loved trees and enjoyed working with wood, I had vague notions of going into forestry as a career. But the school told me it was a waste of time as there were no jobs in that industry for women. The school countered with a suggestion that I should be an art teacher "because I was not good enough for anything else." What a travesty of information! I was naive enough to believe what I was told.

Although a career of some kind was very much encouraged by both parents, my mother still tried to steer me into what she felt was a conventional way of life. She would not let me wear pants as a kid (now I don't even own a skirt) and hinted that marriage was a state to aspire to. She was, however, a strong, opinionated and very independent woman and these were the qualities I was unconsciously influenced by, rather than what she said I ought to do.

It was my mother who found a college she thought would be suitable for me. It gave courses in both horticulture and the dairying industry. "If I had had your opportunities ..." she so often said to me. She was passionate about horticulture. She managed half an acre of garden around our house, growing a lot of our food, and read about the great Victorian gardeners who designed grounds to stately homes. But I was not particularly interested in tilling the soil, and never did any of the work in our garden voluntarily. I didn't want to end up weeding for a career. Besides, tame landscapes never excited me. They could be interesting enough as a piece of art, but they did not speak to me in the same way that wild things did. Groomed paths beside organized vegetation simply had no soul.

I didn't particularly want to learn about the dairy industry either, but the first requirement for the course was to spend a year on a farm and that had considerable appeal. I'd always liked the idea of living with animals—what child doesn't—but my mother had never allowed pets. The drawback to embarking on this path was having to go back to school afterwards, with the thought of "growing up" and "being an adult" hanging like a guillotine at the end of it. There was always a small hope, however, that if I started in that direction, something more exciting would pop up. Many farms took on pre-college students as part of their regular work force then. My mother tried to place me in her preferred southern counties, but I ended up on a family farm near Ilkley in Yorkshire. It was to be one of the most memorable years of my life. Up until then, it was as if I had been living in a room without windows. At Ilkley, I stepped through a door into a whole new world.

....

Tom Mason had been born at Reynard Ing, a two-hundred-year-old stone farmhouse partway up Addingham Moorside in the Yorkshire Dales. He ended his formal schooling at age twelve.

Reynard Ing, the farm in the Yorkshire Dales that launched me into the world.

His wife had a bachelor's degree in agriculture and a diploma in dairying but it would have been difficult to decide who was the better educated. Books abounded in the house and both Masons were dedicated local historians. They had three daughters. The elder two had left home and the younger was still at home. Laura was only eight at the time; I thought she was the luckiest girl in the world to grow up in such surroundings.

Many of the farmhouses in the dale were long, low structures designed to accommodate people at one end and animals at the other. A barn occupied the space in the middle. People used to live in a single room and sleep in the loft above. The Masons' house was one of the last of these to have the three compartments still used in their intended ways, but bedrooms had been added upstairs in the old loft, and a back kitchen had been created behind the main room. The floor was paved with stone, and the roof was covered with massive flags as big as gravestones. The walls were half a metre thick and into one was built a huge open fireplace with a stone lintel. Close by, at about chest high, was another deep niche in the wall, which had been the bread oven. A fire would have been lit in it—there was no chimney and the smoke would have simply gone into the room—and when the stones were hot enough, dough would have been placed directly onto them for baking. The only use for it now was as a favourite nook for the cats.

In the middle of the building was a great arch, big enough to allow a wagonload of hay to pass through. Rickety wooden doors gave access. At the far end was the cow barn, or mistal, with stalls for about eight cows. A larger, more modern mistal had been tacked onto that. The Masons' herd of Guernsey cows numbered about thirty. The farm also had about the same number of ewes, a bunch of chickens in a shed up the field, geese that hung around in the barn porch—at times the gander was ferocious, and I got attacked and pecked quite painfully on many occasions—and the requisite dog and cats. I was enthralled at having all these animals to entertain me, particularly the bottle-fed lambs. I worked twelve-hour days, wallowed in manure, and loved every minute of it. I was always big and strong for my age, and would sling rectangular hay bales until my hands were raw from the strings, and it was I who every morning took the milk churns to the farm gate and slung the fifty-kilogram cylinders onto the waist-high stone platform that stood beside it.

And of course, I walked. The farm was about five kilometres from Ilkley and partway up the side of the valley through which ran the River Wharfe. Farmhouses, even the grander ones, were built of stone, and dry stone walls hedged the fields. The woollen industry had developed in this part of the country; fleece would be gathered in one valley, then horse-packed over the moors to the next to be spun and woven in the mills. I often followed an old packhorse track through farmsteads that seemed to shrink farther into the stony landscape the higher I got, until I reached the moor. (Despite its proximity to Ilkley, its real name is Rombald's Moor.) There I had views up and down Wharfedale, and over the

Studley College, where I studied agriculture.

gloriously empty stretch of heather and bracken beyond. Now a forest of communication towers graces the skyline and people hike up there all the time, but I never saw a soul. If I had gone far enough across the moor and across the next dale on the old packhorse track I would have come to the low stone house where the Brontë sisters had lived. Along the ridge toward Ilkley were the cup and ring stones, petroglyphs from an unknown ancient era, and in the other direction was an outcrop of millstone grit, a kind of sandstone that oxidizes black with age, so called because it was ideal for grinding grain into flour. At one time this outcrop had been quarried, and a couple of round, table-sized stones lay tilted and abandoned below it, half-buried in bracken and heather. There was no road, not even a cart track. How had they taken the usable stones out of there?

Tom Mason had poor health, and no strong sons for muscle power. He taught me a lot about using brains rather than brawn for

Virgins retreat.

moving things around—little tricks like turning an empty wheelbarrow in the direction you are going to take it before it is loaded. Interesting how people never do that unless it is pointed out to them (myself included). About two years before I left Lincolnshire, my parents bought a television. There were only two channels and my parents controlled what was on it, but I easily slid into the routine of skimping on homework so I could stare at the screen every night. At Reynard Ing there was no TV, and I realized what I had been missing: that real life was much more fascinating. I have never particularly enjoyed television since.

. . . .

All things must pass, and with some dread, I presented myself to the college. It was a small one, a converted, not very elegant "stately home," farther south than Yorkshire, where I would be hobnobbing with people from quite wealthy homes. The government gave me a full grant because of my parents' low income.

My mother was visibly relieved to wrest me from the barbaric Dales. All of us, staff and students, lived on the premises. We had a dairy farm and pigs, and we learned to make butter and cheese. Academic subjects included microbiology and veterinary science. I surprised myself by enjoying the classroom work. Horticulture students kept the grounds fairly formal, and we were surrounded by a rather dreary farmland, but at least we were not in a city.

The college was for women only. It was called, of all things, Studley, after the nearby village. The name was made much of by students of Birmingham University who would come a-courting: one wag spray-painted "Virgins Retreat" on the wall of the stone gatehouse.

I made friends at Studley—some I am still in contact with. But during all my vacations, and for many years afterwards whenever I was in England, I went back up to Reynard Ing. What my mother thought of this abandonment of my childhood home she never said but I have never had the slightest feeling of homesickness for it. It has always interested me that people can grow up in an environment for which they have not the slightest empathy. I was not needed in Lincolnshire. My brother had sown a few wild oats in his youth but was now gearing up for a career with my father; eventually, he took over the family business. But there was no way I was staying put. With my college education behind me, my destination was the world.

The Longest Journey
Begins with the First Step

Many of my contemporaries would go into careers in the food industry, but I was more interested in the overseas opportunities pinned to the notice board. I didn't care that they were of a temporary nature; the last thing I wanted to do was "settle down." Canada had always held a fascination for me, probably for the same reason that most North Americans are drawn to Australia. There is an unexplained romanticism to these wide, foreign lands. I had read *Call of the Wild* and *White Fang* and, although I assumed that Canada was, like England, all parcelled up and tamed, I was still drawn there. I was delighted to find a Canadian farm exchange program advertised. The reply to my letter, however, informed me that they did not accept women for outside activities and I would have to work in the house. They must be joking!

VSO (Voluntary Service Overseas, a similar outfit to CUSO) was founded in London in 1958. It sought people skilled in subjects like engineering and farming and promised a life of adventure. With a steady diet of such books as *Born Free*, Africa had been next on my list of places to go. A few weeks after leaving college I found myself at London's Heathrow airport ready to catch a Boeing 707 to Uganda. Planes had been a big part of my childhood, for only a few kilometres from my home an active RAF airbase was situated. The sky above me was regularly filled with all sorts of aircraft, from fighter jets that broke the sound barrier to the absolutely massive V bombers that trundled impossibly slowly overhead. Although their noise was unpleasant, I took them as much for granted as the fields and the dawn chorus. But I had never been inside a plane before. After the passengers had boarded, the *crump* of the door closing was like the locking of a jail cell. I couldn't get out. I was seated beside a fat moustached man, probably already half-cut (I had led a very sheltered life and would not have recognized someone who was drunk), who sensed my nervousness. "Nothin' to it. You need to calm down. Have a double whiskey!" As the only alcohol I had ever consumed was a glass of cider each Christmas, I could not imagine anything worse.

Heathrow is a cramped airport and takeoff is steep. We slipped down the runway just past midnight on Friday the thirteenth. For a moment I was fascinated by the lights of London falling away, but then I became frighteningly dizzy. "Have a double whiskey!" I heard my seat companion roar again. Fortunately, the dizziness soon went, but my heart continued to hammer. I had a window seat and stared out at the darkness. After a short time, my ears became blocked as they do when you travel up- or downhill in a car. But swallowing did not clear them: soon, the blockage became quite painful and I began to go deaf. Faintly, I could hear kids screaming. There was some kind of indistinct announcement, and we landed at Frankfurt, although as far as I knew, this was not originally planned. We touched down well away from the airport buildings and were allowed out onto the runway in the soft, cloudy dark. Gradually, my hearing came back, and after an hour or so we all got back into the plane and took off again. Presumably there had been a problem with the pressurization of the cabin; the rest of the flight was without incident. As I had never flown before, I assumed that both the discomfort and the night walk on a deserted runway were normal. Thank goodness I knew no better!

For the next nine hours, my face was glued to the window. While still in the dark, we flew over a thunderstorm and the pillowy clouds far below us were dramatically lit by lightning flashes. Dawn came as we crossed Italy. The "Boot" was visible in all its entirety in the dim, early light. The sun rose over the Sahara; there seemed to be long streamers of smoke from fires scattered through the desert. What would cause these? There was no forest. Could they be oil wells? Why would they be burning? We touched down at Entebbe Airport late in the morning. The dry, tropical heat was like nothing I had ever experienced before. I was met by some official and driven to Kampala. We passed large quantities of a huge-leaved, vaguely palm-shaped plant. Hanging from the junction of the leaves were great bunches of bananas. I was thrilled. I had no idea banana plants looked like that.

My job was to teach on a farm school near a town called Jinja, whose primary claim to fame was a hydroelectric dam bridging the Nile where it emptied from Lake Victoria. The dam provided power to all of East Africa. The farm school also lay beside the lake, but we couldn't easily reach it as we were separated from it by a wide swamp full of papyrus and elephant grass. We were warned never to enter any water as such country was a prime breeding ground for bilharzia. This parasite has a bizarre life cycle. It needs two hosts to complete its breeding program. One host is a mammal, the other a minute snail that lives on vegetation at the surface of still water. What an amazing creature to need two such disparate hosts. The parasite does not kill, but compromises the health of everyone it infects. It was estimated that 98 percent of the local population suffered from it.

Hippos apparently came out of the water at night, but my clearest memory of the swamp was the frogs. The night chorus was as much of a roar as the dawn chorus had been in England.

The route from England to Australia.

There was so much noise it was hard to pick out the individual choristers. The door of the house I shared with other VSOs stood open during the day, but was always locked at night (a first for me—I had never lived in a locked house before). When the door was opened in the morning (usually by me), tiny, jewelled tree frogs were often to be found on the hinge edge of the door. They would have crawled there before it was shut; in the morning they were squashed flat.

I never saw a lion or giraffe or any other big game, for I never went to a national park, but the invertebrate life around the farm school was fascinating. Flying termite swarms, safari ants, giant millipedes like little model tube trains and of course mosquitos. After I had spent an evening sprawled on the government-issue yellow-cushioned couch, I would rise to find my outline perfectly delineated with squashed bugs.

One of my favourite invertebrates was a spider. Its smooth, black, yellow and red body was the size of my thumb joint, and its thin legs were longer than my fingers. The second pair of legs was even further extended—they could be swung forward and used as antennae. This spider made extraordinary webs that were so huge they often started on a branch higher than my head and were attached at the bottom to the ground. If I inadvertently walked into one (which I occasionally did, such as when we were chasing escaped pigs around a straw-thatched building) I would have to stop to claw the silk off. Twice I released small birds that were fluttering helplessly within the threads.

I easily fell into the position of a delighted observer of the natural world, but it was a different story with my job. I was totally out of my element as far as teaching went. I had found most schoolwork easy—I had been able to read when I was three—so had no memory of the process of learning. Uganda has sixty tribal tongues so the official speech is English, but for many this was a secondary language. The students were all young adults; some would have gone through any university in the world with flying colours, but others could not write a recognizable sentence. I had no idea how to teach them. I did not even have a curriculum. Now, VSO expects their employees to have more suitable skills. I was also put in charge of the dairy herd. The exotic cows had to be submerged in a chemical bath twice a week to rid them of ticks. Naturally, the cows did not like this and many fought the students' half-hearted attempts to push their heads under with poles. Again, I had no experience as to how this should be properly done and the small herd all contracted some tick-borne disease and died. My African career thus ended somewhat ignominiously and I was let go.

Back in England I got a job as a relief milker. I would fill in on dairy farms when they were short-handed. I seemed to have great difficulty fitting into most work situations, though, and was let go twice more. I worked hard, I was a good herdsperson, but employers did not like me. I was mortified by this and didn't know how to rectify it, but I now think it was because I had never learned to be tactful. How lucky I had been to stumble over Reynard Ing. It was still my refuge when I had nowhere else to go.

. . . .

I drifted around for most of two years. One of my college friends was now at university. I stayed with her one night to see a slide show by a famous Himalayan climber. This was before tourism climbing became such a large industry in Nepal so these expedition members seemed akin to gods. Although my own hiking experience was limited to walking the rain-beaten hills in the north of England and Scotland, I had read everything I could get hold of about the real mountains in the world. I had some notions that I would be a climber one day, but this was still very much a dream.

I ate a cheap dinner with my friend and a group of other students. One of these was a man with a beard and coarse blond hair dragging against his collar. The crotch of his jeans was crudely stitched with great loops of thread. My mother would have been horrified that I was even talking to him. "I am particularly interested in this talk," he announced, stuffing execrable pasta into his beard, "because I am going there myself this summer." "Oh, how I wish I could go with you!" I exclaimed. He barely paused in his chewing and said, "The world is full of people who say *I wish* and yet never do anything about it. All you have to do is do it. You can come if you want. I am charging everyone one hundred pounds." He was planning to take a couple of Land Rovers overland to Nepal that summer. Why not? I thought. It was like an epiphany. I suddenly realized I could do anything I wanted. Dreams could become reality. "Why not!" I said to him out loud, and right away wrote a cheque. That young man had unwittingly opened another door for me and I shall always be immensely grateful to him for that. I often wonder what happened to him. I don't even remember his name.

We crossed the channel by hovercraft and drove through Europe, Turkey, Iran, Afghanistan, down the famous Khyber Pass to Pakistan and then to India. I gained some pleasure out of the trip but I was not particularly enamoured of my fellow travellers. They seemed to be totally uninterested in off-road exploration along the way, and preferred to devote their time to procuring drugs. Hard as it is to imagine now, drugs were not universal at universities then, and it was considered very daring to buy hashish once we reached the Middle East. The students preferred to sleep until noon and drive half the night. Scenery, to them, was "boring." None of them were bad people, they were simply frustratingly limited. It was the first time I had done anything with a group for a length of time and I vowed it would be my last.

Part of the students' problem was lack of time. When they reached Delhi, heavy monsoons defeated their attempts to reach Kathmandu and they had to turn right round and go back to Britain. In a tourist campground, I ran into a couple of Australians with a van and travelled for a time with them. We scrambled through major flooding and managed to reach Kathmandu on the only road that existed then.

The road to Kathmandu.

Arriving in Australia.

The very first trekking business had started up several years earlier, but nothing was happening when we were there because of the rains. We tramped around a little bit on some very soggy trails, but the mountains were beyond our reach. Once in a while a tantalizing glimpse of snow and ice floated impossibly high among the clouds.

We touched Thailand (but could not leave Bangkok as the country was closed to tourists in 1971) and a bit of Peninsular Malaysia, then caught a cargo/passenger boat in Singapore for the two-week sail to Sydney. Four months after leaving England, I set foot on Australian soil.

I spent most of a year there, working in orchards or on dairy farms, and did not stray from the southeastern quarter except for one quick visit to a friend on the tropical northeast coast. As always, the wildlife was of great interest: Australia has some of the deadliest poisonous snakes in the world. It didn't stop me sleeping on the ground, a fact that horrified most residents. Australia was where I was introduced to hitchhiking and I spent many a night under a bridge or in a ditch beside the road. I had one or two minor scares but soon learned that it was a most interesting way to travel. I had a one-on-one relationship with my tour guides, who often had very strong opinions about the country we were travelling through.

One of my more memorable hitchhiking forays was up the east coast to Townsville. A friend was living there. I spent Saturday night just north of Brisbane. I crept off the road into a patch of bush in the dark and unrolled my sleeping bag. Not far away, a group was having a party on a deck protruding over the bush. I remember thinking that they would probably freak out if they knew I was sleeping below them.

The next day was Sunday, not usually a good day to hitch-hike as the big transport trucks were not running and families rarely picked people up. I had a few small rides, then came to a corner where another hitchhiker was standing. As well as his backpack, he had a young kangaroo—a joey—with him. It was already as big as a terrier, but would still have been riding around in its mother's pouch so was quite happy to sit in a duffle bag. "Isn't it difficult to get a ride carrying a pet around?" I asked. "Not a bit of it," he replied. "I get rides from families with kids. They see the joey and the kids scream that they want to pick me up." Most Australians have never seen a live kangaroo.

I did amazingly well on a succession of small rides that day, and by late afternoon had covered eight hundred kilometres, which I thought quite respectable. I generally went into hiding about an hour before sundown as the last daylight hour was when the yahoos cruising for a bit of action would be driving around. I would get onto the road again at three or four in the morning; the first truck to see me would screech to a halt. That afternoon, however, I decided to put my thumb out for one more car. The driver was a young army officer, recently home from Vietnam, who couldn't wait to get back into action. He wasn't at all a macho or aggressive person, just lost. Help for war veterans was probably not readily available then and I often wonder if he was able to reconcile himself to peace.

He was to carry me for another eight hundred kilometres that night for a total of 1600 kilometres in one day, which was a personal hitchhiking record. The country was by now largely uninhabited, and ground-level bush fires crawled alongside the road in the darkness. We arrived at his barracks in the small hours of the morning and I unrolled my sleeping bag under a gum tree by the gate. I was up at first light with only fifty kilometres to go. I at once got a ride with a local guy in a pickup. Low morning sun poked golden fingers across the road. And out of the shrubby bush walked a cassowary. He was a male, tall as a man, and resplendent in breeding plumage with his bare blue neck and red helmet or casque rising above his head. My driver braked at once, and we watched this magnificent bird stroll across the road. The driver was as excited as I was. He said he had been travelling this road for twenty years and had never seen one before.

On the whole, Australia did not excite my senses in the way many other places in the world have done, but one four-day hike was to open yet another door. Not because of what I saw, but because of what I experienced. Most of the walk was along an overgrown bush road in a gully at the edge of the Blue Mountains of New South Wales. I had no map and was not very sure of where I was going, but the gully was rimmed by farmland; if I got lost, all I had to do was scramble out of it to reach country that was inhabited. I camped beside a small river among snaky-barked gum trees, and watched ducks and other denizens of the forest with delight. One time I rested on a fallen log and was aware of a movement in the bushes. There was not a breath of wind but the branches seemed to be trembling. I could not believe my eyes. Thousands of leeches were undulating toward me. They were only a centimetre long, but they were all unerringly headed in my direction. They inched to the ends of every twig, their hungry mouth parts circling round trying to detect their prey. I had collected leeches in my socks a time or two in Asia and wetter parts of Australia, but the sheer numbers of them at this spot, and the way they were mindlessly seeking me, was like something out of a horror movie. I might have marvelled at their prey-sensing abilities but I had no desire to continue with the observation and my rest was rapidly curtailed.

On another occasion I glimpsed an animal the size of a small fox. I never saw its head, but the body and the way it ran were distinctly cat-like; unlike with most wildcats in the world, however, the spots on this animal's coat were white. When I asked people about it, they could not imagine what I had seen. Years later, I read about quokkas, recently discovered "marsupial cats." They are not cats at all, having pouches and long-nosed, possum-like faces, but when you see them moving, it is obvious where

My house in New Zealand.

the cat name comes from. All these farmers busied themselves in their "civilized" world above the gully without any idea of the rare treasures that were living next door.

The most exciting thing about this bush walk, however, was not the wildlife but another marvellous personal discovery. I had never before been on my own, out of sight and sound of other human beings, for more than a few hours. I was totally unprepared for the euphoria that four days of solitude gave me. It was completely different from being alone on a simple day hike. I don't understand why this should be so, but it was an experience akin to ecstasy. Are these the feelings people achieve through chemical stimulation? If so, I can see why they are drawn to it. I have no experience of mind-altering drugs: the only stimulant I have ever used is caffeine.

. . . .

Hiking in the Southern Alps in New Zealand. I'm on the left.

From Australia I caught a boat to New Zealand and lived there for five years.

Working on dairy farms, either as a herd-tester or relief milker, I spent all my spare time in the Southern Alps. I made a trip or two with a tramping club to begin with, but was soon on my own. New Zealand is blessed with a network of mountain huts, some as well-appointed as a resort and others crude shepherds' shacks. I would pack food and art supplies for up to ten days and give myself to the natural world and solitude.

I was tempted to stay in New Zealand. It had most of what I wanted—incredible bird and plant life, an easy climate, spectacular scenery—but Canada never quite let me go. I had travelled halfway round the world, mostly overland, and knew if I stayed in New Zealand, I would always wonder what the other half was like. While growing up, I had assumed that everywhere was like the British Isles: that each piece of land, even the "wilder" parts, was owned and manipulated by humans. I thought that I had been born too late to be an explorer and there was no true wild country left. Even my euphoric bush walk in Australia was conducted in country that had once been roaded and logged. New Zealand had also been greatly changed by human impact; before Europeans arrived, the various waves of Polynesians had brought fire and pigs that drastically changed the ecology. But I met quite a number of North Americans travelling in New Zealand. I was beginning to realize that there were unspoiled places in the world, and that people still built log cabins in the woods.

The Other Half
of the World

I planned a sojourn through South America, starting in Panama, with the idea of travelling down the Andes through Argentina and finishing with a promised job on a sheep farm in the Falkland Islands. I knew no Spanish, but had learned Latin and French at school so figured I would pick up the basics fairly well. Mostly I would try to remember the French word and add a Spanish ending and in fact that worked quite well. I was pretty clueless for a day or two, though. I wanted to eat so I stopped at a cheap outdoor place and sat at a table. A chalkboard menu offered half a dozen dishes. I had no idea what any of the words represented. I pointed to the second on the list: *hígado*. Soon a huge lump of tough old cow's liver was put in front of me, all the pipes and tubes still sticking out of it. Fortunately I have a strong stomach and was able to dispatch most of it. Another item on the menu was *corazón*. I learned later that this was "heart."

Most people consider Spanish to be a beautiful language, but I found it harsh (at least, the accents in South America seemed to be). When I could pick out a few words, I would hear passionately romantic songs blaring out onto the sidewalks referring to *mi corazón*, and would immediately think of a great, bloody, freshly butchered organ on a plate. Not quite what the singer intended, no doubt!

I rarely travelled in comfortable tourist transport except when there was no alternative. Hitchhiking was just as expensive as cheap buses or trucks—one had to negotiate the price before one climbed aboard. Andean people are small in stature, and the buses were like our shorter school buses: made for passengers with short legs. I could never sit with my knees forward; they always had to be at an angle. Add to this that a three-passenger seat was often crammed with four or five bodies—well, you get the picture. Times were rarely adhered to. One might wait for hours to get started. Some of the bus journeys lasted more than twenty-four hours. I preferred to ride on top, lounging among the luggage that was held in by a sturdy roof rack, sometimes sharing the space with a couple of sheep tied to the spare wheel. Five-ton trucks with wooden crates on the back were even cheaper than the buses. They carried people, livestock and freight, all jumbled together in the back. Women with children were given places on the freight to sit; the rest of us stood, often for many, many hours.

The roads were incredible. Imagine standing on a high point, chopping up a handful of spaghetti and flinging it over a mountainous landscape. A tiny little curved piece would land here, another there, still another way over there. Somehow, all these bits of road would be laboriously joined together. It would take hours to climb or descend four or five thousand metres. Often the roads were single-lane and many of the vehicles had no brakes. I remember one bus journey of thirty-six hours. The co-driver simply spread out on a couple of seats beside the driver and snoozed. Whenever another vehicle was encountered, the co-driver had to leap out with a rock and put it behind a wheel while the operators of both vehicles argued as to who should back up to a passing point. On one occasion I remember a hairpin bend so tight that even the short school bus had to make a thirteen-point turn to get around it. (And this *sans* brakes!)

I managed a few hikes, mostly on well-used trading routes. I rarely saw other tourists, but locals driving livestock were common. One man rode a donkey, and he was followed by half a dozen sheep. Both cooking pots and live chickens were tied to their backs. Although these other trail users were interesting and colourful, it was always a real treat when I found myself alone.

Maps, if there were any, were crude in the extreme. A single line would show the river; another delineated a trail; a third would join the highest points of the mountains. One had to determine by the number of wiggles and zigzags which line represented which. In Peru, I followed a trading route for a couple of days, then branched off up another valley. I was both surprised and delighted to find myself completely alone.

I was supposed to be on an old Inca trail, but because of lack of use, it was difficult to find. I was above the treeline in a kilometre-wide shallow valley rimmed with a natural rock wall that was flat-topped and amazingly consistent in height, probably about thirty metres above the valley floor. In one spot, there was a small nick in the wall. Had I known that was where the trail was headed, I would have gone straight for it; the ground was easy to walk on, being mostly gravel. I wasted time hunting for the trail, though. In the past I had often been confident about direction and happily abandoned a poor trail, only to find myself in trouble.

Above four thousand metres in altitude, I always slow down, and the pass I was aiming for reached five thousand metres. Progress was therefore very slow. Periodically, huge slabs of flat, glacier-worn boulders littered the landscape. They didn't protrude above the gravel so I could find them only if I came upon them. On some of these were straight lines of head-sized boulders. They were covered in lichen, indicating they had been there for a very long time. No natural force would have made such straight lines; I could only assume that they were ancient Inca route signs. Unfortunately, they were not visible from very far away. They all pointed toward the nick in the wall.

It started to grow dark. I was carrying no water and was a little alarmed about spending a dry night. There was a distinct lack of vegetation so when I noticed a bush behind a rock in the half-light, I headed for it and found a bath-sized pool. I scrounged a few dead twigs to make tea and cook a meal (tea, beans, carrots and onions were my standard fare: they were readily available in the market and I figured I could always eat the carrots and onions raw if necessary). As the light came back into the world in the morning, I saw that the pool was jam-packed with mosquito larvae. Oh well, they had been thoroughly boiled, and they no doubt added nutrition to my vegetarian diet.

Slowly I continued to follow the sporadic lines of ancient stones and did indeed reach the nick in the wall. It was like something out of Tolkien, for suddenly tiny steps (for feet much smaller than mine!) climbed the bottom of the wall and entered the nick. Within two strides, I was through the pass looking down into the next valley. It was breathtaking. A lake lay not too far below. It was motionless in the early sun and it reflected a panorama of mountains. To my right were the great snow and ice buttresses of Huascarán, the highest mountain in Peru. I was to run into a considerable number of people in this new valley, for it was a popular place for climbers. I had no idea of that when I started the hike.

I wanted to sit and savour this wonderful sight. I scrambled onto the top of the wall and sat for a while. Suddenly, there was a buzz. In front of my nose was an incredible creature with a needle beak and helicopter wings. It zipped up and down and sideways. I had never seen a hummingbird before as they don't exist outside the Americas, but I knew at once what it was. What a precious gift at such a fabulous moment.

. . . .

Another notable hike took place in Bolivia. I caught a truck to an open-cut mine not far below another pass at five thousand metres. I was once again following an old Inca trail. The day was late when I arrived at the village where the mine workers lived. The lone teacher at a little schoolhouse said I could shelter there for the night. The only piece of furniture inside was a single table, on which I slept. Presumably, the students sat on the dirt floor. No glass graced the windows, and the local alpacas were rounded up into the schoolyard for the night, where they periodically grumbled and sighed.

I was away early as usual and slowly, slowly reached the pass. Slabs of snow streaked the stony summit; I was standing on the great divide of the Andes and conscious that the melting snow in the direction I faced would eventually reach the Amazon River. I was not alone in this pass, however, although I could see no visible sign of life. But from crevices within the rocks came hollow clinking. I surmised that people were trying to mine whatever mineral was present independently of the big outfit down below. It was very strange: the shaley ground off the trail didn't even register their footprints. The only indication of their presence was their hidden musical tappings.

The Inca trail at that point was more than two paces wide. Occasionally a big rock had somehow had its top taken off—it was possible to see drilled holes radiating out from the centre. The Incas had only soft metals, like gold and copper, so no one knows how the stones were shaped. Around these larger boulders, other flat stones had been fitted with precision. Were it not for the occasional steps in it, one could have driven a truck over this road.

I spent the next night at the start of the vegetation so I could use the scrubby bushes for my cooking fire. The next morning, I went down, down, down. The trail was clear enough, but the old Inca road soon disappeared beneath growth that became more luxuriant as I descended. The climate changed dramatically. For lunch, I ate blackberries; at suppertime, I ate oranges.

. . . .

At the time, the only way to get to the Falkland Islands was via an Argentine Air Force plane from Rio Gallegos. I had been promised employment on a sheep farm for the shearing season, which lasted for the summer. That's how long it took to fleece 500,000 sheep. After that I worked as a teacher for a school year in a settlement called Goose Green. I had a class of eight- to ten-year-olds who were all boarders from outlying islands. Again, my teaching skills were not great but I was good at all the extracurricular activities. We were short of desks so I made some out of old beer crates. Unblocking the sewage was as much part of the job as putting the kids to bed. I loved taking the pupils on hikes to see old shipwrecks and collect penguin eggs. The latter made a nice change to the endless diet of mutton. Even a small penguin has a large egg; if you collect it early in the season, the bird will lay another. Penguins are feeding on krill when they are breeding, and as a result the yolk is as red as the crustacean. The white, however, stays opaque. A boiled egg (takes fifteen minutes) looks, therefore, like a large bloodshot eye. A fried egg fills a pan and resembles a half-melted plastic bag. They taste like slightly strong hen eggs.

The Falklands are an archipelago of mostly treeless peat bog with a few stony hills here and there. It is a wildlife paradise: five species of penguins, elephant seals (how soft the young ones' coats are!), sea lions and a variety of very interesting birds including a large, flightless sea duck that moves by windmilling its short stubby wings against the water like a paddle steamer. They are known as steamer ducks. The Falklands War (of the Thatcher era) happened after I left; many of the places I used to hike are now out of bounds due to the plastic landmines laid by the Argentine army. War is really so stupid. Plastic means the mines can't be detected, and there was no record of their placement. Presumably the wildlife and the sheep will eventually set them all off and render them safe.

. . . .

Before I left New Zealand, I addressed a letter to "The Canadian Embassy, Wellington," stating that I would like to enter their country in about two years' time. I got a letter back from the Canadian embassy in Sydney, Australia, saying they could not process the application until six months before my immigration date but to please drop in and see them some time. No cheap flights operated out of New Zealand then. Full return fare to Sydney and back would have cost a fortune.

Eighteen months later, in the Falkland Islands (which was, and still is, a historical remnant of the British Empire and therefore listed as a colony) I wrote to "The Canadian Embassy, London, England." Surely they would have one. I received a reply from Buenos Aires. "We cannot process your application until you are guaranteed a job. But pop in and see us some time." Going to Buenos Aires from the Falklands was just as expensive and difficult as going to Sydney from New Zealand. While in the Falklands, however, through a contact I had made in New Zealand, I did manage to secure employment with the Canada Farm Labour Pool, dependent on getting immigration. Canadians, it seemed, did not like to milk their own cows.

After three months in southern Patagonia (incredible glaciers; guanacos; agoutis; condors; rheas; armadillos; monkey puzzle trees) I finally walked into an actual Canadian embassy in Santiago, Chile. The man at the front desk was a local. My Spanish was never very good and the Chileno accent was hard for me to understand, so we talked in English. I tried to describe that I was in the process of applying for Canadian immigration and he said: "How long have you been in Santiago?"

"Two days."

"You have to be in Santiago six months before you can apply for Canadian immigration."

"But I have already started to apply," I replied. "I am hoping that there are documents waiting here for me."

"Where did you apply?"

"Buenos Aires," I replied, keeping my fingers crossed. Chile and Argentina were having a war at that time and all inter-country transactions had deliberate, pain-in-the-butt, monumental delays.

"How long were you in Buenos Aires?"

"Two weeks."

"You have to be in Buenos Aires six months before you can apply for immigration to Canada."

"But Buenos Aires was only the nearest embassy. I was living in the Islas Malvinas!" I called the Falklands by their Spanish name. "I was there a year and a half!"

"Who," said my erstwhile interrogator, "owns Islas Malvinas?"

My heart sank even further. What side was Chile on in this debate? "The British say they own it," I explained. "Argentina says they own it."

That stumped him. "Moment," he said. He left his desk and shortly ushered me into the office of a real live Canadian. I showed him the document promising me work if I could get through the bureaucracy. The Canadian had me fill out a form of things I could do in the agricultural world and he was blown away because I said I could drive a tractor. Of all my skills, that was what impressed him most. But he told me that the next stage of the application was to pass a medical examination and it would likely take so long in Chile that I would be better off going back to England.

I was heading north by that time anyway, although a return to England had not been in my plans. The postcard telling my parents that I would be visiting them arrived after I did. (My parents didn't have a phone.) Once there, I went through all the steps, and four months later flew on a standby to Seattle and then a short flight, in the middle of the night, to Vancouver.

The Call of the Wild

I had picked western Canada because I had looked at a map and found that's where the mountains are. The Farm Labour Pool that had sponsored me into the country was in Armstrong near Salmon Arm in southern BC: not exactly Jack London country anymore, but a good enough place to find my feet. Dairy farming in Canada, however, was not what I was used to. I was given only the most menial tasks and not encouraged to have any interest in the running of the dairy herd. I was not supposed to calve difficult cows, feed the calves, manage the breeding, determine what they should eat or do any minor veterinary procedures, all of which I had taken care of in New Zealand, and which made the work interesting. The farm was supposed to be state-of-the-art for Canada, but I found the set-up antiquated. In New Zealand I had operated six or eight milking machines at once, which had kept me on my toes. Here I had only four; milking 120 cows took four hours twice a day. Most of the time I was bored out of my mind. Another two hours were spent cleaning up. That was all I was supposed to do. To make matters worse, the milking parlour had no windows and I was never outside. I might have been in a factory making widgets. No wonder Canadians had to get immigrants to do the job.

Accommodation was part of the wage and I was given a trailer to live in. Some people might have been pleased with a shelter containing all the mod cons, but I hated the artificial surfaces and dreary layout. Everything sweated in the cold. The location was not particularly nice, either. The Trans-Canada Highway, with its constant flow of traffic, ran on one side of the farm, and the railway hugged the property on the other. At night, trains blew their whistles a few hundred metres from the trailer and their brilliant headlights glared into my sleep. I had arrived in Canada at the beginning of November and I survived the winter in this trailer, but by spring I had moved to other farms and work was more sporadic. By then I had managed to acquire a tiny frame hut that had been designed as a sauna. It was more crammed than the trailer had been, but it was real—and it was mine. I built a couple of extensions and managed to squeeze a floor loom into one of them. I had learned to spin in New Zealand and when I was not working on a farm, I created yarn, dyed it with plants and wove garments for sale. I also started painting scenes—old barns and the like—and managed to sell quite a few pieces. One way or another, I made a scratch living.

The little shack was twenty minutes west of Salmon Arm and two kilometres from the Trans-Canada Highway. I was fairly high up the valley side and had a clear view of this road; sound travels skyward and my world was rarely free of the noise of traffic. In two years I never learned to ignore it.

I was leaning toward having some kind of farm—sheep, rather than cows—and had some notions of building my own cabin in the wilderness, but all this was very vague. I had been to Vancouver and Banff, but I had not yet travelled north. The BC road map showed a highway running west from Williams Lake. Most of it seemed to be unpaved (this was 1981) and there appeared to be hardly any people living on it. It looked more like my kind of country. Salmon Arm friends told me about a couple who homesteaded off-road close to the western end of

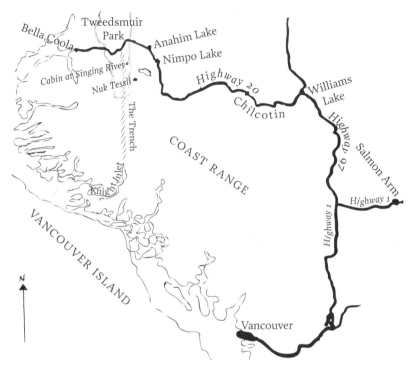

Sketch map of the Chilcotin.

the highway. Books had been written about them. My friends, who had also been pioneers and who were now actively retired, had hiked in to see this couple. They had offered the homesteaders their horse-drawn tedder, a machine for fluffing up hay to help it to dry properly. At present, the homesteaders were doing this job by hand, which was very time consuming. The tedder would have to be taken into their place by float plane; for that, they would use a charter company based at Nimpo Lake, four hours' drive west of Williams Lake. "I bet you could get that tedder into your pickup," my friends said, and that was how I met the Turners.

. . . .

The Chilcotin is the name given to that sparsely inhabited chunk of land between the Fraser River, just west of Williams Lake, and the spine of mountains that runs parallel to British Columbia's west coast. The thin thread of Highway 20, some of it still quite rough in places, joins Williams Lake to the small town of Bella Coola at the head of a long inlet that enters the open Pacific Ocean one hundred kilometres farther west. Highway 20 is 457 kilometres long, not all of it paved, and in good conditions it now takes about seven hours to drive. Bella Coola, population 1,800, is the second-largest community west of Williams Lake; the other half-dozen places are little more than a post office-cum-store-cum-gas station, although a couple have RCMP outposts and three have clinics and schools to grade nine.

The Chilcotin is dry at the eastern end, sometimes grassy, but gradually it becomes covered with Douglas fir that, as the climate becomes harsher, succumbs to scrubby lodgepole pine. Most of this rolling plateau is volcanic. Remnants of the mountains that created it poke above the plateau at intervals, particularly toward the western end, but the whole Chilcotin is one vast field of magma many metres deep. Much of it is now covered with a layer of silt and gravel deposited during the last ice age, but numerous outcrops of the strange five- or six-sided basalt "organ pipe" formations, which are classic volcanic features, hug the plateau's rim.

Highway 20 climbs gradually from Williams Lake. Until the late 1940s, it ended at Anahim Lake, which is now a little over four hours' drive west, although at that time it was a journey of at least two days. Between it and the Bella Coola Valley are dramatic mountains, which then were breached only by trading routes travelled on foot. The Bella Coola people had wonderful resources: fish, meat, timber with which to build houses and boats, plants to make fibre and various wild vegetables and fruit. In the interior, people led a much harsher existence. They sometimes walked down into the Bella Coola Valley to fish, but mostly they hunted caribou. They did, however, have one very important resource. Obsidian is a natural volcanic glass, which can be split into shards that are sharper than any man-made substance. These shards were invaluable for arrowheads and spearheads. One of the items from the coast that the interior people coveted was the fermented oolichan oil that was prepared by the Bella Coola people. The trading routes became known as grease trails.

In the late 1940s, businessmen in both Anahim Lake and the Bella Coola Valley petitioned the government to link the two communities overland. The problem was the great wall of mountains in between, and the government said a road would be impossible. Locals took matters into their own hands. One man rode on horseback and marked a route with flagging tape; others followed, from both ends, with Caterpillar tractors. Eventually a small amount of government money was allotted to help complete the road. The Cats nudged blades in 1953 on a section that even now clings to a steep mountainside by the skin of its teeth. That part is still single-lane.

Although the road is much improved and extremely well maintained whenever it is physically possible, it is still a wild mountain highway. The difference in altitude from top to bottom is about 1,200 metres; some of the hairpin bends necessary to achieve this reach grades of 18 percent. No barriers prevent the eye from careening over the precipitous drops, and erosion and avalanches happen with every big rain or snowfall. Locals call this stretch of Highway 20 "the Hill." At the top is the high, dry, cold Chilcotin; at the bottom, the warm, wet Bella Coola Valley.

The bottom of the Hill marks the northern tip of a vast, deep trench that runs south for 250 kilometres, eventually tumbling into the ocean at Knight Inlet. The headwaters of two rivers are spawned in a big swamp in the middle of the trench. The Klinaklini River flows south; the Atnarko River runs north, entering the

Bella Coola Valley at the bottom of the Hill. The trench is steep-sided and its base is low enough to be coastal in climate. It is choked with tall cedars, Douglas fir, spruce and birch.

The Bella Coola Valley is about a hundred kilometres long. In 1912, the road ran along about two-thirds of it. The legendary pioneer Ralph Edwards trapped along the Atnarko River, and forty-five kilometres from the end of the road and about twenty-five kilometres into the trench he found a place he figured was suitable for a homestead. It was at the head of a ten-kilometre-long body of water that wound between the mountain spurs. He spent many years alone hacking down the large trees with a handsaw and an axe to create enough open ground for a log shelter and a garden. Solitude was a way of life for many pioneers, but Ralph did not always enjoy it. He named the place Lonesome Lake. His inventive life was documented in a book that has been translated into many languages: *Crusoe of Lonesome Lake*. Other books have followed.

Eventually he found a partner to share his lonely life and they had three children. Trudy was the youngest, and also the only girl.

The homestead had water, good soil and a reasonable growing climate, although frost-free days in summer were never guaranteed. The higher Chilcotin plateau, however, was much drier and colder, and Ralph saw a way to make a bit of income by shipping his produce to the resorts that were beginning to emerge on the dozens of lakes that covered the western end of the plateau. Overland travel would take too long—the produce would rot before it got there. Flying was the only answer. When Trudy was in her late teens, she was sent to the coast to get her pilot's licence, buy a plane on floats and fly it home. For a year she transported produce to the resorts. Then her father obtained his pilot's licence—he was already in his sixties—and took over the flying; Trudy never piloted a plane again.

Trudy's two brothers, John and Stanley, left home in their teens and spent most of their working life outside. Trudy, however, wanted nothing more than her own homestead. She walked even farther up the Atnarko River, found the first reasonably flat place, and started handlogging to clear her land. Jack Turner, a surveyor who also enjoyed solitude, heard about this renowned young woman and decided to walk upriver to make her acquaintance. On a subsequent trip, he brought a chainsaw and left that tool with her as a promise of intent. He came back and married her.

....

The Turners had homesteaded for over thirty years when I came upon the scene. They had a tight house and barns, tame-grass hayfields, bridges and fences and an extensive garden. They kept horses to do their lifting and cows for meat and milk, and added fish and game to their diet. Apart from the chainsaw and a motor for their boat on Lonesome Lake, they had no gas-powered machinery. Everything that they could make themselves, they did: shovel and wheelbarrow handles; shafts and boxes for wagons; hinges for the gates. With no sawmill to cut their lumber, they relied on hand tools to split or carve the wood.

One August morning I arrived at the float plane base at Nimpo Lake with the tedder in the back of my pickup. Correspondence with the Turners had been by post office mail, and as a thank you for bringing the machinery, they had invited me to fly in and visit. The tedder would have to come on a later plane as the iron wheels would need to be strapped onto the floats' struts and pilots did not like to carry such awkward external loads and passengers at the same time.

It was my first flight in one of those overgrown bumblebees. Little did I know how much they were to become part of my existence. With my panic level off the scale (I have never been able to get rid of my flying phobia) we took off from Nimpo Lake and droned over the rolling forest of the Chilcotin. Suddenly, the land fell away into the great north/south trench. The plane spiralled down on a wing to lose height in the narrow valley and hissed onto the head of the lake. The Turners' homestead was another five-kilometre hike through the forest.

I spent a couple of memorable days there, eating horsemeat and drinking home-canned raspberry juice, and then the Turners walked me to the highway. They kept a boat on Lonesome Lake, and also on the Stillwater, a much smaller lake a few kilometres downriver. This sped up the journey considerably, even though many hours of hiking were still necessary. The Turners invited me back "any time," and I right away said I'd love to see the swans.

Trudy's father, Ralph, had made outside income by trapping, and also by guiding hunters. All wilderness dwellers did that in those days, and many still do now. One of Ralph's clients, an American named John T. Holman, liked to shoot bears. A common way to do that at the time was to note where a grizzly was denning under the snow for the winter, then dig him out and blast him. Ralph found a den and sent a letter to the client, and eventually the American turned up with guns at the ready. People with modern sensibilities may be shocked by this little-known story about the legendary Ralph, but it was considered perfectly normal behaviour then. It was documented by Holman in a book published in 1933 called *Sheep and Bear Trails: A Hunter's Wanderings in Alaska and British Columbia*.

Holman's visit was to have far-reaching effects for the inhabitants of Lonesome Lake. He was a naturalist as well as a hunter, and he noted a handful of swans by a small bit of open water where the river ran into the lake. He recognized them as trumpeter swans. Once common over much of North America, they had been shot almost to extinction to make pens from their wing feathers and powder puffs from their down. Holman and Ralph applied to the Canadian government to start a feeding program for the couple of months the swans would be wintering in the valley. Ralph horse-packed in the feed.

Ever since she was a little girl, Trudy had taken on the job of walking out onto the ice with sacks of grain and feeding the birds. When she staked her own claim up-valley, she continued with this task. The swan flock increased exponentially, reaching a maximum of five hundred birds, although when I arrived, around one hundred was a more common number. This amounted to an awful lot of grain. Trudy's book, *Fogswamp*, details the huge task she and her husband and young daughter, Susan, completed every year in moving the grain from the end of the road to the head of Lonesome Lake. Between the lakes, the feed was carried on horseback; around them, trails were poor or non-existent, so the horses had to be transported on rafts. As there was no fodder in the forest, hay had to be carried for them, too, and food for the three Turners also had to be planned. It took weeks. When the first float plane company started up at Nimpo Lake, the grain was flown in. The Turners staggered the flights throughout the year so they could receive mail and library books at more frequent intervals.

The best time to see the swans was in January. Thus the second time I flew into Lonesome Lake, it was in a plane equipped with skis. Where the Atnarko River runs into the head of the lake, it has built up a narrow bank of willows for about a kilometre. This bank almost walls off a chunk of water, and the resulting pool is known as the lagoon.

Swans have elegant long necks, but these are not designed simply for humans to enjoy. They have evolved so that the birds can grub about underwater without having to dive. The water, however, must not be too deep for them to reach the bottom. Plants and insects do not grow in fast-flowing water; relatively still shallow water that is still open in winter is not easy to find. Such a place occurs at the bottom end of the lagoon. The Turners had built a shed by this spot and it was here that the grain was stored.

It turned out, when I arrived for the winter visit, that Trudy hadn't been well, and she wanted to see a doctor. Jack said that if I could look after the place alone, he would be able to go out with her. Of course that was no problem for me. I kept the fires going to prevent the Turners' food from freezing, fed and watered the animals, milked the cow and of course walked down to the lagoon every day to feed the swans. I felt not the slightest qualm at being left so far from human help in such a wild place. Obviously I wished no harm to Trudy, but to say I was ecstatic at being alone in this romantic, dramatic and magical place would be an understatement.

To Reason Why

Until people started asking me why I wanted to live so far away from communities, it never occurred to me that my desire for such an existence needed an explanation. Isn't literature full of the beauty and peace of nature and the horror of overcrowding and pollution? Or do other people not read the same books as I do? If that is the case, why do so many of them decorate their walls with representations of natural landscapes such as wildlife and sunsets? They presumably receive some benefit from this somewhat soulless reproduction of the world beyond their walls. Only an artist who enjoys abstract forms and colour would want to live with a depiction of industry.

If people agree that nature is pleasing, why do so few want to live in it? Is it the work? The lack of conveniences? Fear? Fear of what? The dark? Wild animals?

City folk live a schizophrenic existence, however. At the same time that some corner of their mind accepts the necessity of nature for both the health of the planet and their own sanity, they are also groomed to look at any place beyond city walls as backward and "uncivilized." Literature is just as full of those kinds of references as well. My kind of life, city folk postulate, is not the "real" world. Which means, presumably, that reality is composed of artificial building materials; artificial light; an artificial climate; artificial fabrics; an artificial calendar that bears no relationship to seasonal or circadian rhythms; artificial entertainment; artificial plants; artificial food and chemical-enriched water. Such "reality" seems to be synonymous with "civilization." My world is directly involved with creating my own warmth and shelter, organizing my own power system, obtaining food and water and disposing of waste in an ecologically acceptable and safe manner. Is this not a real world? I might wear pitch-stained, ragged clothes and sleep under the stars or on a park bench at times, but I don't consider myself uncivilized. I know how to be polite. I don't even swear all that much. I am well educated and reasonably intelligent, and I don't drink alcohol or smoke any kind of drug; I am responsible, reliable, caring of others' property and sensibilities and, although I follow no recognized religion, consider myself to be spiritual. I am even glad that cities exist: without all the technology that they represent (books; publishers; the Internet; chainsaws; toilet paper; this computer) my life would be far less rich. I am also glad that most people prefer to live away from the wilderness—otherwise it would become too crowded. But if people ask me why I choose to live this way, I find it difficult to explain to them. Isn't it obvious? Or do we really exist on such different planets?

While I was staying at Reynard Ing in Yorkshire, I once read an article in the *Countryman*. It was translated from an Italian publicity brochure from 1977.

I look at these images of houses … made of stone, straw or snow and I wonder what emotions they stir in a townsman.

I think that the townsman looks at them with longing and anger, with the feeling of having been wrong in everything … [H]e dreams of a house in the country … with no television or telephone, where to grow sage and rosemary, where one can bury oneself whenever possible … to get disintoxicated from atmospheric and human pollution.

Then, when he can buy his hermitage [and] tries to bury himself, ... on the third day he is back again offering impossible justifications, when he is in fact only upset by the loneliness and thoughts which come when he is alone.

But the moral is that, for the townsman, his [hermitage] is situated in a sort of spiritual geography: simply by thinking of it, it materializes, together with the sage and rosemary and the silence ... But he has not got the nerve [to live in it], and ignores the civilization that makes a person choose this kind of life ... [H]e finds it easier to fight at a meeting than to fight alone against a long winter or a summer heavy with storms. [H]e feels more comfortable in a traffic jam ... than driving a tractor in the fields, where there are no traffic lights, and nobody on whom to discharge his own neurosis ...

[One] day we will have to thank the countryman who remained there to guard the peach tree, the silence, and the smell of hay. To show us that the starting point is also the point of arrival.

I suppose the best way to explain my choice of life is to state that when I discovered solitude I found myself. When I am alone, experiences are so much more intense. After that first solo hike in Australia, I knew that solitude was going to be an important part of my life. Before I had experienced it, I could never get on with people very well. Afterwards, I could enjoy them; only, however, if I had repeated doses of being truly alone.

It is not because life in the wild is simple, as is so often fondly imagined by the city dweller. They are the ones who have it easy. They do not have to figure out how to create their shelter and warmth, supply themselves with water or acquire food in a place with no stores. Wilderness dwellers are as much constrained by the laws of the land as city dwellers are, and they are much more conscious of the laws of nature as well. Despite this, there is a freedom of spirit to this life that very few city dwellers will ever experience.

Of course I am frightened of bears at times, or the weather, but my greatest terrors are getting into a plane or driving on a freeway. I guess we are most comfortable with the dangers we are used to. I cannot imagine living with the overwhelming tensions and noise of a city; city dwellers cannot imagine fending for themselves alone in the bush. But who has the most dangerous life? All I can say is I am not the one who locks my doors.

....

Jack and Trudy were away for most of a week; fortunately Trudy's medical problem was soon resolved. I had naturally mentioned to the Turners that I was interested in building a cabin somewhere in the woods. They of course didn't think this wish unusual. When Trudy and Jack returned, they asked if I would like to build on their property. They were getting older, Susan had left home, Trudy's father's homestead was now uninhabited and they were in fact more isolated than they had ever been.

Their offer caught me totally by surprise. There I was, a thirty-four-year-old woman with a rural English background, being accepted by the pros. To have the means of consolidating my dream given to me so easily was completely unexpected. Interestingly, it was not my wilderness experience, love of solitude, hiking capabilities or handiness with tools that impressed the Turners. To them that was a normal part of life. The skill that made them think I could fit in was my ability to milk a cow. That is where I differed from all the other wannabe wilderness-lovers that had crossed their path. One would think that a career linked to dairy farming would have produced a pedestrian life, but milk cows have opened a lot of unexpected doors for me around the world. I will have to write a book about that some day.

So I tidied up my life near Salmon Arm, packed all my possessions into an old Dodge three-quarter-ton pickup with a

Outside the old sauna, packed up for Lonesome Lake. Photo by
Gudrun Hupfauer.

homemade crate on the back and drove to the float plane base.
It would be a month before Nimpo Lake was open and the
summer flying season could begin so I dropped off most of the
freight, then continued down the Hill and walked up the river to
Lonesome Lake.

It was April and the forest beside the river was fresh and sweet
with the newness of the year. I could drive a very rough road for
about ten kilometres—it took an hour—then it was up the trail
over the "ding-blasted bluff" that Ralph and Trudy had dynamited
wide enough to carry horses loaded with packs. My young dog,
Lonesome, pranced the trail with me. I had acquired her as a pup
from one of Trudy's brothers when I had visited the Turners the
first time. The trail brought me to the widening of the river known
as the Stillwater. There was no path for the next two kilometres,
and I had to pick my way over the boulders of a steep rockslide.
Between the Stillwater and Lonesome Lake was a stretch of dark
cedar forest much inhabited by grizzly bears, although I saw none

Beaver float plane at the Turners' dock. Trudy (left) and Jack Turner.

on that trip. They would have been newly out of bed and munching the new growth at the bottom of the Bella Coola Valley.

Just before Lonesome Lake, a wild stream spews out of a narrow cut in the valley wall. It comes from an extensive high lake chain before tipping over the valley rim in a thousand-foot drop known as Hunlen Falls. This creek can be very difficult to cross during the spring flood, but that was weeks away and in April I barely got wet feet.

Around Lonesome Lake there was a bit of a trail but it was no longer well maintained, and it was full of windfalls. Eventually I reached the lagoon and the swan grain shed, where I spent the night. I lingered over my camp in the morning, enjoying the breathless beauty of the lake; from there it was a comparatively easy five-kilometre hike to the Turners' homestead.

Cabin at Singing River.

All my food and building supplies could be flown into the lagoon, but they had to be carried up the trail to the homestead. The Turners helped me a lot with this. We all used backpacks, but most of the heavy items were loaded onto horses. I spent many an hour plodding behind a massive-footed, continuously farting gelding called Lucky. It was June when the main building operation began; the river was roaring with runoff, birds were brimming with hormones and deciduous greenery was soft and lush with spring. I was given a building site across the river from the Turners' house. They had tried to grow grass there but it had never taken so the site was consequently of little use to them. I established a long-term camp a short distance downstream, well away from any trees I might accidently fell in the wrong direction, and the following day, with great trepidation, I took my new and shiny chainsaw to the location of my first wilderness home.

I Become a Writer

When I was at Lonesome Lake, an event happened that changed the focus of my wilderness career. At first I had vague notions of being self-sufficient, like the Turners, while gaining a meagre cash income from the sale of artwork. But on a mail trip from Lonesome Lake, which I tried to manage once a month, I picked up a letter from a friend who suggested I write to Peter Gzowski. He was a well-known host for *Morningside* on CBC Radio, a three-hour show every weekday from 9:00 to 12:00. Often listeners' letters were read on the air. They were about almost any subject one could imagine; Peter Gzowski was a most eclectic interviewer. I used to hear the program when I lived near Salmon Arm, but couldn't receive a signal in the trench.

I think while I hike, and composed many missives in my mind as I strode over the trails, but it took six months before I had the courage to put one on paper. "*I live 25 miles from the nearest road and 75 miles from the nearest store. I built my house with logs cut from the forest …*" I sent it off, but had no contact with the outside world until I reached the post office again a month later. All of Bella Coola was talking about it. "We heard you on Peter Gzowski!" I received a message to phone the producer. "Do you want more?" I asked. "Yes," was the emphatic reply.

This was heady stuff indeed. I was no stranger to writing letters for I had been sending them to my mother ever since I left home. I had also been keeping journals for many years. But to have my scribblings broadcast across the country was incredibly exciting. I had no idea they would be such a hot topic. At first I sent them on every mail trip. They were aired regularly, and several were published in Peter Gzowski's own anthologies of listeners' letters. Twenty-five years later, people still tell me they first heard about me on this program. (It shows how old we both are.) A magazine called *Harrowsmith* was extant at the time. It catered to back-to-the-landers. Emboldened by my success with Peter Gzowski, I sent in a couple of articles. This was pre-Internet days and we polished them by phone on my once-a-month mail trips. No editor would have the patience to do that now. What an ego boost to see my work in print! And they paid well, too.

On the air, it seemed like I was Peter's best buddy. He also wrote a letter to me, praising my writing and stating that if I ever put a book together, he would be pleased to contribute a foreword. But in fact we had little to do with each other. He publicly boosted my image but privately, he was a stranger. I had no problem with this. He was a very busy man overloaded with human contact. I understood completely how draining this could be.

The idea of writing a book was not new to me, but putting it into practice was something else. I would start off with great enthusiasm; day two's effort was more of a grind, and by day three I usually fizzled out. Two years' worth of letters, however, was enough material to make a book-length manuscript. All I had to do (I naively figured) was create a few paragraphs to join the ends of the letters together and I would be set.

At the time, *Harrowsmith* was owned by the same company that published rural living books under the Camden House name. I reckoned I could wave Peter Gzowski's offer to write a foreword under the publisher's nose like a flag, but I didn't feel confident enough to approach the man himself. I sent a draft of the Peter Gzowski letters to Camden House along with a copy of Peter's promise. I called the book *Cabin at Singing River*.

Camden House was obviously reluctant to publish it; if it hadn't been for Peter Gzowski's name, I would not have got anywhere. There was a long gap while the publisher contacted Peter and waited for his reply. Finally, the news came back. Peter told the publisher that he would indeed write a foreword as promised, but they would have to fork out $1,200 to use his name. That was a lot of money in the late 1980s. This payment, however, was not to go to him, but to me. I was to receive it upon publication.

Needless to say, simply joining the radio letters together with little paragraphs was not going to work. The material needed a complete restructuring. A wonderful editor took me through the process and I learned a great deal about writing as a result. In all, I reread—and often rewrote—the manuscript thirteen times. I was using a typewriter so each draft was laborious and time-consuming. I typed the final piece on a friend's home computer, one of the first I had ever seen. When I received Peter Gzowski's bonus, I bought my own computer and a small solar-powered system to run it. *Cabin at Singing River* was instantly on the Canadian bestsellers list and continues to be a favourite to this day.

. . . .

Instead of pursuing the idea of subsistence farming, therefore, I began to travel around in the fall, and sometimes in the spring, to promote my art and book. I illustrated the talks with slide shows. People might think that staying for a month in push-button homes, with access to running hot water, indoor flush toilets (with *warm* seats!) and all the other city amenities would be a nice rest for me from life in the bush. But it was just as tough a way to make a living. I hate the noise and the stink of cities, and the driving on busy roads and freeways, especially on winter nights. I also found having to work in the evening exhausting. And, worst of all, I was never alone. Had I not known that there would be an end to the tours, I could never have done them. For all that, I love public speaking. Who can fail to enjoy showing off in front of a large audience, who then proceeds to tell them how marvellous they are?

AND THE RIVER STILL SINGS 71

One question I am often asked is how I can marry this very public face with my need for solitude. Well, I certainly could not do the former without the latter. But I think it is more than that. Without wishing to appear boastful, I think I know myself. Someone who is at home with their persona, no matter how good or bad, has confidence in their abilities. Whether that person goes into the bush and builds cabins single-handedly, does heart-transplants, goes round the world in a wheelchair or stands in front of hundreds of strangers and spouts does not matter. If you think you can do it, you will.

The Queendom

The wildlife at Lonesome Lake was superb. I have never lived anywhere else that provided such variety: everything from moose to caddis fly larvae, from bald eagles to western toads, from wolverines to American dippers, from herons to river otters—and of course, grizzly bears. A great deal of the activity centred around the river, especially during spawning season. The Atnarko was a major breeding ground for five different species of Pacific salmon. Each species chooses a different part of the river to perpetuate its life cycle. Chum, coho and sockeye stay lower down, while the springs and humpbacks travel farther up the river. I thought it curious that the springs, which are the biggest, spawn where the river is smallest.

It was the sockeye that came to the Stillwater, Lonesome Lake, and the Turners' homestead. This fall bounty attracted an enormous variety of creatures, not just grizzlies, but trout that fed on the salmon eggs, ospreys and otters that fished the trout, mergansers that ate the salmon eggs as well as the smaller fish, and bald eagles who thieved from everyone. Bears love nothing better than rotting meat or fish, and they were thick around the river during spawning season. Their trails ran in the forest right behind the cabin. I would sit on the porch on a dark, late-September evening and hear grizzlies slopping around the shallow water after the flapping fish, barely a stone's throw away. Hikes to the road meant an encounter with at least one or two bears. I had a few frights, and the poor dog, Lonesome, was terrified, but mostly the bears were just as keen to keep out of our way as we were of theirs. I even fell over them in the dark once in a while and, with great crashings in the bush, they galloped away. Ironically, after the Turners later moved to the Bella Coola Valley, Jack was severely mauled by a grizzly. He was very lucky to survive. Lonesome Lake will always hold a significant part of my heart, but I was not destined to stay there. It was not really what I wanted. I like to be in the high country. The trench was deep and steep-sided and it was a very long, rough hike to get into the alpine: there was only one trail, an old surveyor's route that climbed up from the head of Lonesome Lake, which meant that if I wanted to go in another direction I had to bushwhack. Up the rocky, steep sides of the valley, this was very hard work. I am also a dawn and sun worshipper, but the valley's narrow profile meant that sunlight was limited—on the short winter days, one could see its golden glow on the far mountains, but it reached the cabin for only two hours.

Then the Turners started talking about selling their homestead. I couldn't afford to buy it and I didn't know how long the sale would take or who the eventual owner would be. Would I still be allowed to stay?

In the meantime, such explorations as I had been able to manage had taken me above the treeline in all directions. I had a single 1:50,000 topographical map. Lonesome Lake was at the top; in the southeast corner was another lake about which I started to dream. I had none of the charts beyond this unnamed lake, and it was so close to the edge of my map, I could only guess at the surroundings. Judging by what I had seen on other hikes, however, I figured there must be a pretty good view of the Coast Range. It also looked as though a squarish point on the northeast side would not only be well placed visually, but also have good sun exposure.

First I had to get there to have a look. As I knew nothing of the country beyond the lake, it seemed logical to try to get there from my existing cabin. The Turners had built and maintained a trail beside the river for about twenty-two kilometres up-valley from their homestead. It petered out in a horrendous swamp. The Turners took their horses up there for the summer when they were not needed for haying. They had never been interested in finding a route to where I wanted to go, so once their trail ended, I was on my own.

My trusty map (a very ragged piece of paper at this stage) showed a spur that looked a little less steep than the rest of the valley wall and I headed for that. First, however, I had to cross the swamp. House-sized willows with horizontal branches as thick as a human leg joined hands over car-sized hummocks and pools. My dog, Lonesome, an expert packer by then, could not get through with her load on so I strapped it on top of mine. I frequently had to take my pack off as well and push it into a gap ahead of me; the branches fought me every step of the way. At last I reached the east side of the trench and found the creek that ran beside the spur, and then my luck changed. There was a game trail up the spur so well used it was worn twenty centimetres deep in the duff. Near the top of the steep bit, the land became rockier and the game trail was much harder to find. Windfalls added to the difficulty. Some of the rocky steps were too steep for a pack-laden dog to manage, so once again I periodically carried Lonesome's. However, the game trail was obviously the only way up and down the valley for many kilometres in either direction. On the bluffs were goat, deer, bear, wolf, and even moose tracks and droppings; I would not have imagined moose being able to climb rocks where I needed my hands as well as feet to make progress, but they obviously could.

Above the bluffs, the country levelled out and the trail disappeared. From there on it was a long, slow, uphill slog fighting slide alder and misery bush for many an hour. Although I am

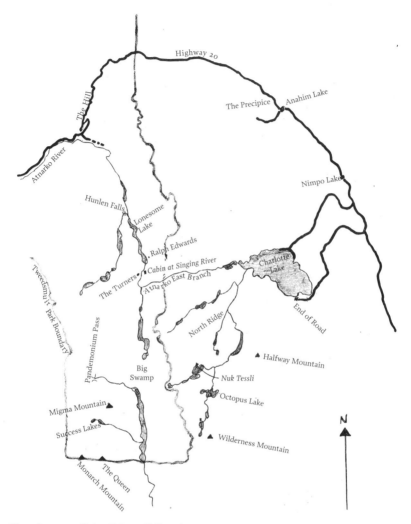

Sketch map of the West Chilcotin.

a good map reader, I have no sense of direction and I never did learn to use a compass. I needed to stay within reasonable distance of the creek to find my bearings. The creek made a jog and I knew I could have saved time if I'd taken a direct line, but the country was featureless otherwise. On later trips, once I knew where I was going, I made much better progress by travelling in more open country farther west.

At last I reached a height of land and began, almost imperceptibly, to go down. I came to a straggly shallow lake whose waters were now heading east instead of west. There it was, on my map. It was not the end of my journey—there were two more lakes to get around—but the country had undeniably changed. I had crossed the great divide and was now on the rolling, forested plateau of the West Chilcotin. The trees were at once smaller, more subalpine; the land sloped more gently and was sodden with swamps and mudflats. There was no recognizable trail. I fought my way along the shoreline and at the foot of the little lake I could see the magnificent mountain view I had hoped for.

Finding a campsite was not easy in that country, which was either boulders, dense tangles of subalpine fir or swamp, but I spent the night on the shores of the second lake and reached the squarish point I was aiming for the following day. The second night I put my little backpacking tent on a tiny patch of sedge near the point; it did not face the sunrise but there was no other place among the boulders with enough space to lie flat. I made a tiny fire at the edge of the lake. From my temporary kitchen, I could look straight toward the mountains. They were high and, although it was then mid-August, they were covered in snow and ice. A hard frost occurred that night; when daylight came, my camp and the sedges were white. But when I walked to the other side of the point, the sun was hitting it, just as I had visualized it, and I was instantly warm. The view up the lake, the orientation to the sun and the wildness, was everything I had imagined it to be.

I couldn't allow myself to think that the place would actually be mine. I didn't see how the government would let me build there. There was no harm in going through the motions to stake a claim, however. It didn't cost very much then. When I was next in Williams Lake, I went to the Land Office (now the Land Title and

Survey Authority of British Columbia) and asked for the form. I filled it in and sent in the fee. Then I waited.

. . . .

In the meantime, I packed all my possessions back down the rocky trail to the swan grain shed. The Turners kindly put them on empty grain planes. In fact, they found a buyer for their place about the time I left. It was taken over by the Tweedsmuir Provincial Park, which already surrounded the property. When private property is bought, park policy is to let the inhabitants stay there as long as they want, but the Turners decided to retire into the Bella Coola Valley. Jack moved into a trailer on his daughter's farm, where he could watch television to his heart's content, and Trudy bought acreage over the road and built herself another cabin. She was in her sixties by that time. She and Jack were always together and supportive of each other—Trudy gave Jack milk from her cow and Jack helped her with chainsaw work. They just preferred to live in separate buildings.

I spent a summer in the arctic, and a winter in a friend's rough little cabin only fifteen kilometres from the nearest road (what an easy hike that was!). I signed up for the first of what would be eight springs as a tree planter. I would need that money to outfit myself for my new adventures in the wilderness. Then the next lot of government forms pertaining to the claim I had staked arrived.

Part of the process involved "planting a post." I obviously could not just drive along there and pound in a pole. The form came to me at the end of summer and, as each process seemed to take three to six months, I said I had already staked it. I did not think anyone else would go there and claim it first. By that time I had got to know the family who were trapping in the area. Jealously guarding their trails and shelters from usurpers, they were in fact very generous to me with information on routes and the locations of their rough little cabins. They of course didn't come into the area from the Lonesome Lake direction; they travelled on horseback or snowmobile from Towdystan, which is not far from Nimpo Lake.

My lake.

I figured early April would be a good time for me to approach the claim along that route. I knew I would be able to find the trappers at their winter base, which was about halfway between Nimpo Lake and the claim. Their winter cabin was at the eastern end of Charlotte Lake, the largest body of water in the area. The north side hosted a number of cabins and shacks that were joined to Nimpo by dusty bush roads, but the south side was forest. I could have driven to the cabin if the road had been open, but it was well packed with snowmobile trails so the hike from the highway took only a day. The trappers had come out of the mountains in early March, when the ice on the lakes and rivers could still be relied upon. I reckoned I would be able to follow their old snowmobile tracks for a good part of the way.

I left the trappers' cabin shod with snowshoes and with five days' worth of food and camping equipment. I dragged some of it behind me on a toboggan; Lonesome carried her pack as well.

People have often asked me why I never hitched my dogs to a sled, but dogs need a relatively flat and broken trail to work effectively. Although I would have a ready-made trail on this trip, that was not to be the case most of the time. The country I traversed was hummocky, rocky and full of trees, and the snow in sheltered places was deep and soft. It was far more efficient for me to break trail while dragging a toboggan loaded with light and bulky stuff like sleeping bag and axe, and have the dogs carry the heavier food and cookware on the flattened snow behind.

The trail I was following on that journey loosely paralleled the river that ran between the nameless lake and Charlotte Lake, and was buried in forest all the way. Because the trappers had been along it not long before, most of the windfalls had been cut out, but the area had been affected by the pine beetle and every time a wind blew, more trees fell over. There were places where I did not dare follow the snowmobile tracks onto the ice, because the river had broken up considerably since they had been by, and for those stretches I had to tramp my own trail. But the days were long, the weather kind, and I made good time. On the second day I crossed the frozen lake to the rocky point on which I had stood eighteen months before. "Planting a post" was of course impossible among the frozen rocks, but I tied a note wrapped in plastic to a tree right on the corner of the point. I had packed a tape measure along, and I strode out the dimensions on the ice. The government forms had told me to use two-hundred-metre increments, which I did: two hundred metres on one side of the point, then two hundred metres on the other. When I eventually sent in the forms, however, the powers that be flung their hands up in horror and said, "You can't have all that waterfront!" This despite the fact that the nearest cabin was on another lake fifteen kilometres away. They cut me down to "a third of a hectare, more or less," an area just big enough for the two cabins I proposed.

Four days after leaving the trappers, I arrived back at their cabin. Six-year-old Patrick ran out to greet me. "Did you get there?" he said. When I nodded he said, "Wow! We never thought you'd make it!" So I guess his parents had been discussing me after I left. And I don't doubt that a forty-year-old woman with an English accent who had not been too many years in Canada must have seemed an unlikely candidate for finding her way around in the bush in winter. But I had never, at any time, felt uncomfortable or out of place. It already seemed like home.

....

The 1988 tree-planting season ended in early July and I again hiked to the claim from Charlotte Lake. This time, I was planning to stay. The river route I had used in winter would have been miserable with swamps and windfalls, especially as I would have had to fight my way around all the lakes where there were no trails at all. I had more maps by this time and I gambled on an alpine hike instead. Managing to slither my way through a couple of horrendous bogholes, I took the road to the now untenanted trappers' cabin. A day's snowshoe trip now took one hour.

I followed a horse trail up a creek. At first it was easy but soon it became so overgrown I lost it more often than not. But the valley was narrow and I couldn't mistake the way. The bugs were terrible—far worse than they had ever been at Lonesome Lake. I had no bug protection and broke off a spruce branch so that I could whack it around my head, like a horse's tail, every step of the way. After fighting slide alder and spruce swamp for a while I gained the treeline, which, as the valley was north-facing, dipped low. I camped beside a little creek that ran out of a small lake, a tarn really, in a spot that was to become a favourite of mine, even after an avalanche knocked most of the twenty-centimetre-thick, hundred-year-old trees flat several years later. The smoke from a smouldering fire gave blessed relief from the bugs.

The next morning I left the remnants of the trail behind and climbed around a shoulder of the mountain. This peak was more or less in the middle of my hike and I eventually started thinking of it as Halfway Mountain. I stayed high until I could see a great

Lonesome and me on Halfway Mountain looking toward the Coast Range, my lake in the middle distance.

panorama of snow-covered peaks. Nestled among them was the high lake that I hoped was to become my future home. The wind beat at my face and made my eyes water. "The Promised Land!" I yelled into the wind. The dog looked resigned.

The last part of the journey was a bushwhack plunge down through tangled subalpine fir that gradually opened into the pine forest surrounding the lakeshore. I had not been exactly sure how long the hike would take me, but I was well within the two days that I had allowed. I had booked what would be the first of many, many planes for day three.

Listening to the lapping waves while waiting for it the following morning, I seriously considered that the first plane might be the last. On the initial trip during that perfect August weather nearly two years before, I had eyes only for the view. Drifted over with snow in the winter, the ground had looked comparatively flat. Now every distorted tree, hollow, bump and boulder was revealed in graphic detail. Was I really going to be able to move logs over this inhospitable ground? At Lonesome Lake, I had help with hauling and lifting. I had neighbours to give me advice when I ran into problems. They supplied me with food before I was able to grow my own. Here, there would be no gardening. The ground was too rough for a wheelbarrow, let alone a horse.

What perversity made me keep my mouth shut I don't know, but when the plane came, I said nothing to the pilot. The green canoe I had learned to paddle in on the lagoon at Lonesome Lake was strapped to the plane's floats. I used the boat to ferry supplies from where the pilot could drop them (not a lot of choice in this supremely rocky shore) to the place I had chosen for a camp. The first thing I needed was a stout crate to protect supplies from bears. I fired up the chainsaw and that first alien man-made mark was made.

Nuk Tessli

I had searched for solitude, and I was to enjoy plenty of that at the nameless lake. The longest I ever went without seeing or speaking to another human being was to be seven weeks—and this was B.I. (Before Internet.) Cyberspace has completely changed solitary living. But when I built those first two cabins, I never dreamt that such a service even existed, let alone would be available to me.

At Lonesome Lake, I had built on private property, but the nameless lake was on Crown land, and the Canadian government would not let me simply put up a cabin and live there. I had to have a commercial reason. The only thing possible in this high, rocky landscape was tourism; the only tourism niche available was for hikers and naturalists. Even if I had wanted to deal with horses and guide hunters, the outfitting rights in the area were already taken.

I had to sign an agreement for a backcountry recreational lease with the BC government and Her Majesty the Queen of England. They required a management plan, and I proposed two cabins, one to live in and one to accommodate guests. Being such a loner I was somewhat apprehensive about committing myself to a tourist business, but, as I have so often done before, I put any unpleasant thoughts about the future out of my mind. It would be a good while before such a business was functioning, and I would enjoy the preparation phase in the meantime.

The come-along, the most useful tool I had.

The guest cabin was to be smaller and I tackled it first. It was not the building itself that took the time, but the finding, felling, peeling, preparing and hauling of the materials. It was Trudy who showed me how to move and lift heavy objects, such as logs, using levers and blocks and tackle. This was to stand me in very good stead. Right at the beginning of my wilderness career I "borrowed" a come-along from good friends in North Vancouver who had used it to build their house. I still have not returned it: it has been one of the most useful tools in my possession.

The ground around the nameless lake was either boggy or hummocky and covered with large, coarse-grained boulders. Partly because of this, partly because I was working alone, and partly because this upper montane forest provided few good building materials, I chose a modified *pièce-sur-pièce* method of construction. For the walls, lodgepole uprights were placed about two metres apart and short logs or half logs, usually whitebark pines, were slotted in as fillers. Most of these could be dragged through the boulder field with a rope, one tug at a time, but I needed longer logs for the foundations and the roofs. Hauling a ten-metre-long tree could take all day. I would lever one end up in order to put a roller underneath it. This involved placing the lever (either a peavey, or just a thin pole) in the correct place, holding it down with a foot and manhandling the roller beneath. A real yoga stretch! The roller wouldn't actually roll because of the rocks, but it would lift the log off the ground and therefore reduce resistance. I did the same at the other end of the log, then fitted a third roller in the middle. Next I would crank the come-along and move the log until it snagged on something. The distance gained might be two or three metres, but often was no more than a few centimetres. I would work the come-along until the rope was guitar-string tight, then nudge the log with the peavey so that it jumped over whatever was stopping it. Back to the come-along again until either the log jammed once more or the cable ran out and the whole thing had to be reset. I did a lot of muttering and exclaiming moving some of those big logs. (Not talking to anyone else does not preclude talking to oneself.) When the log was coerced far enough forward to drop off the rear roller, the back end would land on the middle one, and I could move the rear roller into the front.

Lifting the logs onto the building structure was easy enough but a tedious process. It involved erecting complicated scaffolding that was very time-consuming to make—particularly as I had to build a ladder before I could work on anything higher than I could reach.

So I felled trees, peeled logs, cut them to lengths, hauled them painful centimetre by painful centimetre, swatted bugs, swore at the chainsaw and talked to myself and the dog. Once a month I hiked out for mail. On the initial trip from Charlotte Lake I had camped for a night, but in good conditions I was soon able to reduce the hiking time to fifteen or sixteen hours, which I often managed in a single day. I always carried a camp with me, though, just in case. Sometimes I deliberately made the trip longer for I was experimenting with different routes. I would carry loppers and sometimes even a chainsaw and camp for an extra night so that I could spend a few hours brushing out a trail.

During my earlier visits to the lake, I had not realized what a terrible force the wind could be. The tiny spot I had camped on when first gaining the point that long-ago August seemed the most practical place to put a permanent firepit: I wanted something that would be washed clean by the lake as it rose in the spring so that when I no longer needed it, it would soon look natural again. I used a flat stone that was already clear of water in July, but which, judging by the tide mark of driftwood, needles and pollen, would be covered at high water in the spring. The view from the firepit was glorious. Sometimes the lake was still and the reflections of the mountains were awe inspiring, but all too often, especially in the afternoon, the wind coming from the mountains blew as a strong breeze and many times a gale. I would hunch over the fire in the evening, trying to baffle the wind so that the flames were not driven away from the bottom of the cooking pot. If rain was falling, I would allow the smoke to get inside my coat and warm me. Living alone, I did not care what my clothes smelled like! The tent (a larger one for a more permanent camp) was pitched farther back into the forest. I found a spot that was not exactly flat, but by curving my body around boulders and using another for a pillow, I was quite comfortable. The tent was roofed with a tarp that extended some distance over the back to create a space to store tools. Even away from the waterfront, however, the wind flapped and battered the fabric, driving me nuts with the noise.

Although I had a few basic tools, there was no one to give me advice on any building problem that might arise. Trudy Turner, however, had taught me well. Most people who choose to live in the wilderness have an inventive streak, but Trudy's father had ideas for projects far beyond those of the usual bush dweller and all of his offspring carried on with that tradition. Unlike me, Trudy enjoyed building. For Jack it was a chore that he uncomplainingly helped with but had no real interest in doing except as a means to an end. I could certainly identify with that. Thirty years after I started I am still creating structures and I still dislike doing it, but it has always been the only way I could afford to have what I wanted.

At Lonesome Lake, the Turners knew when I was leaving on a mail trip or a hike, and when to expect me back. They had a radiophone that gave them emergency contact with the outside world. At the nameless lake I didn't even have that. I continued with the monthly mail trips, telling someone at Nimpo when I was planning on coming out again. I was always very careful to make sure I was not overdue. I did not want anyone to send out a search party for no reason.

Three short months after I arrived there, a violent storm gave warning of the long winter to come. It was very much driven home to me how puny my efforts were at creating a shelter. The storm woke me at night. I had just tacked windows into the cabin wall facing the lake, but they were not properly installed and I feared for their safety. By the light of a flashlight, in silver rods of pouring rain waterfalling off the roof, I nailed boards over the windows. I stumbled back to the thrashing tent for my foamy and sleeping bag. There was a stove already in the cabin, so far unused, and a floor, and the roof covered most of the living space. There was no door in the frame or chinking between the log fillers, and soon a regular drip plopped onto my sleeping bag. Trees crashed down all around and there were times when I thought the shuddering building was going to go as well. Three days later, however, when the wind eventually died, the cabin stood firm. It has survived many subsequent storms and looks a little weathered, but the doors and windows still open and close without fuss, which would indicate that nothing major has shifted.

On the mail trip after the storm I contacted a teacher of the Carrier language at the Anahim Lake School. I wanted a suitable name to describe my new home. *Nuk teszli* means "west wind." I simplified the spelling to Nuk Tessli.

The name was for the tourist business, the Nuk Tessli Alpine Experience. The lake, however, remained officially without a title for many years. The trapper had called it Square Lake. Locals never warmed to Nuk Tessli, and my own surname was even more difficult for them to cope with. Some called it Chris's Lake; others, sniggeringly, Spinster Lake (which I thought was quite funny when I heard about it, and I would have been quite happy to make it official). Eventually it seems to have been landed with Whitton Lake. The river that runs down to Charlotte Lake is known officially as Whitton Creek. Another lake downriver used to have this name (it is even marked as such on old maps) but pilots started calling that one Banana Lake due to its shape as it was seen from the air. Land Office documents referred to it as Square Lake on Whitton Lake, which was even more confusing. I simplified things and called it My Lake.

After the wild windstorm, when the main room of the cabin had been made snug and weatherproof, I sat by the darkened window, a single candle guttering on the sill and a sheaf of ragged paper in my hand, and poured my heart out to *Harrowsmith*. The account of my achievements became a four-thousand-word feature article that was nominated for the National Magazine Awards. The editors were particularly interested in how I was able to move the logs around alone, without benefit of heavy machinery. They subtitled the article "Log Building for the Single Woman."

By the time I left to attend a couple of craft fairs that first fall (where I attempted to sell cards and hand-made block prints as well as my book), I had a small, sturdy room that would shelter me when I could get back home. I would have to wait until the ice was good enough to land a plane on: I could snowshoe in at any time, but I couldn't do very much without food and supplies. I house-sat for friends for a couple of months then came back into the mountains at the end of February. I used the winter route that I had taken before, but the trappers had not been operating along the river that year, and I had to break my own trail all the way.

When I started off, it was barely freezing. On the second day a cold front came down and the temperature plummeted. Fortunately the wind was behind me; the chill factor must have been extreme. I staggered to one of the trappers' cabins where at least I could be out of the wind. No kindling had been left and I had to split some. I was not aware of being excessively cold, but my hands were so stiff I could hardly hold the axe.

And when I came to light the fire in the tiny tin stove, I thought I was done for. I couldn't make my fingers bend enough to hold the match. By holding my right hand with my left and with great concentration, I managed to get the match to strike. Fortunately, the fire caught at once. Gradually my body came back to life. It was far from warm in the cabin, however. Most of the moss chinking was missing and the only place to sleep was on the dirt floor where the air was coldest. Even though I kept the stove going, every time I opened my eyes the liquid on the surface of my eyeballs felt stiff and gluey. I stayed there the following morning until the sun was well up, and the rest of the journey was without incident. When the pilot flew to my cabin the day afterwards with a bunch of food and supplies, he told me the temperature had reached forty below. I was ill-prepared for such conditions, and certainly had not expected them so late in the year. I was lucky to get away with it.

I had envisioned being able to amass more building materials during the winter, but heavy snow and bad overflow on the ice meant that it was too difficult to move anything very far. So I simply enjoyed myself and began to explore. For the first time I travelled above the treeline on the ridge behind the cabin and was overwhelmed at the hiking possibilities presented to me. I spent a glorious month in my cozy shelter and snowshoed out high over the mountains at the end of March, ready for the spring tree-planting season.

The Unknown World

Rather than finish the first cabin when I came back to Nuk Tessli the following July, I immediately started on the second. I could live with Cabin One the way it was and the season was so short that I figured it was more practical to do all the outside work while the climate allowed it. So once again I felled and peeled and hauled trees and laboriously raised them into place. I had the shell up before I left for my book tour in the fall, so was able to do a lot of the interior work during the winter. Although it was by no means finished, it was far ahead of both Cabin One and the dwelling I had made at Lonesome Lake, and it seemed quite luxurious when I moved in. I transferred my possessions into Cabin Two at the end of March, just before I had to go out for the next tree-planting season.

Summer three saw a frantic struggle to finish the porch roof and the attic gable ends of Cabin One in time for the arrival of my first paying guests. I had been using the space for storage, but I filled in the gable ends, lined the steeply sloping ceiling and installed a floor. It made a somewhat cramped but usable sleep area when the three downstairs spots were full. Friends of mine were the first clients, and only one other party of tourists turned up that year. During the following winter, I set up the small solar power system and computer I had bought thanks to Peter Gzowski's generosity, and wrote the first draft of *Diary of a Wilderness Dweller.* It covered the time during the building of the first two cabins at Nuk Tessli and was published a couple of years later. It was another instant bestseller.

....

During my decade of wanderings, I had travelled through quite a few of the areas that had been marked "Unexplored" in my brother's *Times World Atlas.* They were all tidily parcelled up and mostly named by the time I got there, but now I unexpectedly found myself in the position of being the explorer I had always envisioned. Sure, the trappers knew the country supremely well, but their horse and snowmobile routes were not always aesthetic enough or even suitable for my purposes, and I don't doubt that I stood on places where no human had gone before. Certainly nothing was officially known about the biology or geology of the area then. Various surveys—fish, wildlife, plant and geology— have been completed since.

My expertise became alpine plants. I learned to understand taxonomy in the arctic because my camera broke and to record the flowers, I had to draw them. This taught me flower structure, and taxonomy instantly made sense. When I arrived at Nuk Tessli, the excellent Lone Pine series of field guides did not exist. I possessed a very detailed but dated British book (most of the Latin names have since been changed) and a tourist's basic wild-flower guide to Alaska. I could only begin to figure out what grew in my backyard.

As I received very few visitors of any kind, I could spend a lot of time exploring. The most obvious direction to tackle first was the ridge north of the cabins. When I canoed out onto the lake I could see a long series of naked bumps poking above the treeline. The problem would be finding the best route up there through the forested areas. The trees were quite open, but underneath was a mishmash of scrub, boulders and windfall, and most flat areas were swampy. Although I had snowshoed over quite a bit of the country during the winter, most of the surface of the ground had been hidden. It remained to be seen whether any of the winter routes would be suitable for the summer.

The first attempts were scrambles over boulder and fallen tree, but at last I pieced together sections more conducive to hiking. Some were on gravel, dotted about with small, tough plants; other areas were covered with tight carpets of heather and crowberry. Higher up, the country opened out. A series of loosely joined meadows cut a wide swath through mats of subalpine fir and boulder fields. The meadows were a bit boggy but the sedges were short and lawn-like, so they were easy to hike over. The last one, which I called Long Meadow, followed a creek that produced a wonderful progression of wild flowers from mid-June until late August.

For me, the most exciting part of a mountain hike is the point at which you burst forth from the forest and have the clean and distant world at your feet. The devil knew what he was doing when he took Jesus up the mountain to tempt him. At the top of Long Meadow, a knoll lifts itself above the surrounding tundra. Below, the forested land swoops down to Nuk Tessli, then climbs the far side of the valley to end in a plethora of snow-streaked peaks, most of which are unnamed. The North Ridge undulates in the other direction, but in between the knoll and this naked ridge is a plateau of tundra and boulders flattened by ice during some indeterminable past. A geologist once told me that the shelves that so often contour the mountains right around the treeline in this area are remnants of a much older ice age than the last one.

The highest point of the North Ridge is far to the right, but immediately in front are a couple of hills that look the same size (although one is in fact farther away and quite a bit bigger). They both have slightly convex sides and little bumps on the top. A perfect representation of a woman's breasts. I toyed with naming them the Goddess or some such, for a while, but a client took one look at them and immediately said, "The Mammaries," and the name has stuck.

The Mammaries.

The Mammaries, I was to learn over the years, boast quite a variety of rock alpine plants, such as alpine harebell, alpine forget-me-not, silky phacelia, alpine goldenrod, mountain avens, various saxifrages and sedums and three species of cinquefoils. The plateau in front of the ridge is watered by a number of springs and the resulting wet meadows are great areas for the standard calendar-picture flora: lupins, paintbrushes, arnica and valerian. These wet spots became known, inevitably, as "The Mammary Meadows."

So now I had two major routes going in opposite directions: one to the road and one to the North Ridge. I eventually worked out several smaller trails, including one all around the lake, but two others also climbed to the treeline. Both were across the lake from the cabins. One could walk around the water to reach these trailheads, but it was easier to get there by canoe. Hiking starts had to be early, though; otherwise paddlers might have to fight the wind.

One trail was twelve kilometres long. It starts along the route to the road, then branches off and goes up to what has become

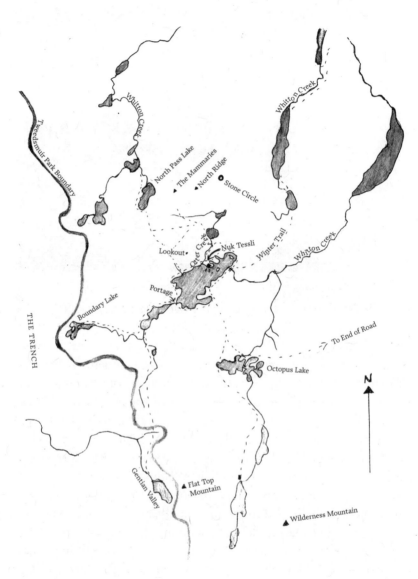

Sketch map of trails around Nuk Tessli.

Wilderness Lake.

known as Wilderness Lake, it being directly under Wilderness Mountain. This is one of the few peaks with an official name on the map. It required several attempts to find a route up there as the country is full of lakes and wet areas, and it is impossible to go in a straight line. I have no sense of direction so unless the sun is shining, or I can see recognizable peaks, I simply go round in circles. Wilderness Lake is only about 120 metres higher than Nuk Tessli, but it is at the edge of the treeline because of the big shadow that Wilderness Mountain casts in winter and the tremendous winds that occur there, the valley being at exactly the right angle to benefit from *nuk tessli's* wildest blasts.

A little higher is yet another lake hemmed in by a long wall of a moraine. Into this a sprawling glacier falls. On my first trip up there, ice caves lay along the bottom edge of the glacier. No one who has never seen ice like that can imagine the range of blues, from palest azure to midnight black, that occurs

The moraine lake above Wilderness Lake.

with every layer of depth under the glacier. The ceilings were melted into points from which water dripped in counterpoint, each note more hollow as the cave burrowed under the ice. In a few years, these caves were gone, but it is now very easy to walk onto the glacier there.

Some years, the moraine lake is still mostly frozen even in August; one time I saw a wolf carrying a young caribou's head as it crossed the ice. It kept putting the head down and looking at us (me and my dogs), then picking the head up and trotting off again. The caribou's ears were flopping. At that time of year the wolf was likely taking its prize back to a den with cubs. Other years the lake would be thawed but icebergs would float in it. Scoop up a cup of water, and it looks clear, but from a distance, it is a dirty greeny-grey, full of a silt so fine it is held in suspension. The silt is made by the relentless grinding of the ice on the mountain beneath. The interesting thing is that the colour of a lake full of glacial silt can vary a great deal. Some lakes are dull green, some emerald, some turquoise and some peacock blue.

A few years after I had started Nuk Tessli, a resort at Nimpo Lake flew in a log cabin to the shores of Wilderness Lake. Naturally I was not particularly happy to think of someone despoiling "my" wilderness, but the owners of the resort had been good to me so I made no protest. The original outfitter had been similarly annoyed when I started building Nuk Tessli, although it was some years before I found this out. Like me, he had no legal claim to anything outside the terms of his lease, but those of us used to vast spaces and solitude don't want *anyone* else to clutter it up. City folk cannot comprehend this attitude and are appalled by our "selfishness." Part of it is a desire to see the wilderness remain unspoiled, but all wilderness dwellers become possessive of their vast territories.

The site for the resort's cabin had been chosen in winter, from the air, when everything had been frozen and covered with snow. The ice goes out there about a month after Nuk Tessli, and the lake was only recently open on the July 1 weekend when the building project was to take place. It was immediately obvious that the chosen site was a bog, but at the foot of the lake was a sandy mound conveniently free of any troublesome vegetation. It had a spectacular view of the great wall of Wilderness Mountain and several ice-hung peaks beyond. There was a reason for the lack of plants at this point, however—it was the windiest spot on the lake.

The cabin had been pre-built in a log-building yard. Lots of people with planes brought in the smaller components, and the bigger logs were slung below a helicopter. A friend and I hiked up there with a three-day camp to see the fun. There were plenty of bodies around to manhandle the numbered logs into place and the whole thing, including the steep metal roof, was put together over the weekend. The classic design for such cabins is with the

Snow bridge in Gentian Valley.

door and main window facing the view. A roof overhang of three or four metres does duty as a porch. I wondered how that con-figuration would work for that supremely windy location—my doors and porches are all in the lee of my buildings, which does create an ice problem at times, but I always felt they would be safer that way. The builder was a professional, however, and he had installed everything from small cabins to mansions all over the world, many of them at high altitudes.

The roof blew off the following winter. When I hiked up there afterwards, I found ragged clumps of yellow fibreglass insula-tion and twisted sheets of metal for half a kilometre behind the cabin, some of which didn't emerge until August when the last of the snowdrifts melted. A new roof was put on and the cabin was braced more firmly to its foundations. It seems to have sur-vived these repairs. It is not a comfortable place to be in during a bad storm, however.

Gentianella tenella.

The third major route I developed was to a less spectacular spot, but for me it was very exciting. Another lake, not quite as big as the one on which my cabins sit, lies upriver from Nuk Tessli (every valley in this country is full of lakes). I had cut out a portage between the two, laying down logs across it so that canoes could be pulled through. The trail starts at the head of the second lake and goes up Flat Top Mountain.

The name that I gave the mountain was an obvious one—from the cabins at Nuk Tessli, it seems to consist of a large, high, dead-level plateau. It lies between Wilderness Lake and Nuk Tessli's valley, and it is possible to get to the Wilderness cabin by going over Flat Top and picking a way down a very steep gully.

Several rocky bumps nudge up above the back of the high plateau. Enclosed by the two at the farthest end is a small, north-facing valley where the snow lies late. A wild creek, often bridged by snow in early summer, tumbles down from a tiny alpine lake.

The walk up the valley is pretty in itself but there are gems in store for those who venture farther. The shores of the tarn are mostly steep and it needs a bit of a scramble to get over them. On the west, the shadiest side, they are topped by permanent snow overhangs. These pour waters down the mountain walls all summer, and every cascade and tiny rock ledge is home to an amazing variety of rock alpine plants, some quite rare: alp lilies, pygmy buttercups, a cinquefoil I have been unable to identify and which I have found nowhere else. One of these treasures is a tiny gentian—*Gentianella tenella.* It is common in Alaska but, as far as I can tell, has been found in only one other location in BC outside Kluane Park.

I have been to a herbarium in Victoria and they do have a few specimens labelled as *G. tenella,* but they are in fact the much more common *G. amarella* (which, incidentally, grows all over the Chilcotin). Birders love to have amateur input, but botanists are a stuffy lot. I have told a number of professionals about my finds but they are never recorded on official lists because I do not have the right letters after my name.

The Third Cabin

N*uk Tessli: The Life of a Wilderness Dweller* was published in 1999. It was a sequel to *Diary* and described the next several years of my life in the wilderness. A little before it came out, I decided I wanted another cabin. I still didn't have an excessive number of clients, but it seemed they always wanted to come at the same time. When I first saw the property on that long-ago August hike from Lonesome Lake, I thought I would build the larger cabin, which would be my house, right on the end of the point, where I would receive the best of the sunrises and the views. But the winds that beat Cabin One during that first winter made me choose a site with more shelter for the second building. Now that I was more familiar with the place, and had watched the way the winter storms blew the snow about, I decided that maybe the top of the point would be feasible after all. It was somewhat sheltered by a massive pile of boulders and a small island just offshore.

I was not sure if a third cabin would ever materialize, however. I dreaded the thought of going through the building process again. I was now fifty-one years old. Menopause was kicking in with a vengeance. I thought that the increased chronic aches and pains I was experiencing were part of the aging process, but clients ten years older than me, whose physical lifestyles could not even begin to compare with mine, were running rings around me. (It was to be several more years before I was diagnosed with food sensitivities and fibromyalgia.) But right at that time, a young man named Nick Berwian popped into my life. Cabin Three would soon become a reality.

....

A wilderness dweller's life is made much easier by having an outside base. All the earlier settlers had someone to stay with when they went to deal with their mail. While I lived at Lonesome Lake and hiked out to the Bella Coola Valley, I stayed at Stuie, not far from the bottom of the Hill, with Katie Hayhurst and Dennis Kuch. I kind of invited myself there in the first place, but we have become lifelong friends. They lived too far away from Nuk Tessli for me to use their place on a regular basis, though.

The closest inhabited community to Nuk Tessli was Nimpo Lake. Early on I made the acquaintance of Gloria Fulsom. She and her husband, Roger, owned and ran the Wilderness Rim resort until they retired, and for several years this became my outside base. Gloria and Roger lived in a low, old log house, which was crammed full with kids and grandkids at Christmastime, and I was always welcomed to these activities.

But I started to accumulate *stuff*. Outside clothes. Income tax records. A vehicle. Unsold books and artwork. Living out of a backpack as I had done while travelling round the world was but a distant memory. Gloria's attic was getting a tad crowded. A rough little cabin was for rent at the other end of the lake. It had two saving graces. One was the owner, who was kindness itself, and the other was the price: it was dirt cheap. Otherwise, it was pretty awful. The cabin had been built on a bog, and as the ground froze and thawed, the building heaved and shifted so the door either never shut, or could hardly be opened. The picture windows had cracked, and the joints in the logs had sprung apart allowing ingress to forty-below temperatures during the winter and clouds of mosquitos in the summer. The skylight leaked, no matter how many times it was repaired, but the cabin was dry

Nick Berwian.

at the other end, and it had a wood stove and a power source to plug in my computer. I had no plumbing and had to haul water from the owner's house. But I could hole up in there and answer mail and wait for suitable flying weather.

I was now presenting fall book tours on a regular basis. They generally ended about the second week of December. Occasionally the ice on Nimpo Lake was strong enough to use as a runway then, but often it was after Christmas or even into the new year before someone would put skis on his plane. I still travelled over-land to Nuk Tessli (even if I had no flying phobia, I and two dogs would take up plane space that I could ill afford) but I always needed the aircraft to fly in supplies.

I rented that cabin for fifteen years, but did not like being there. The neighbours were few, but they were the hunting, snowmobiling, yard light, satellite TV crowd and I had little in common with them. Days were alive with machines, and the nights destroyed by artificial light. I spent as little time there as possible. I would extend my tours abroad by staying with friends, often working for a while for my keep. A favourite place to visit was Black Creek, an hour and a half east of Williams Lake. Artist friends had a farm with gardens, sheep, dogs, horses and cats, and there was always a lot of work to do. A glorious river flowed below the property, and the surrounding wetlands pro-vided fascinating wildlife, including wolves and cougars who periodically ate the sheep. I dug the garden, sheared the sheep and butchered lambs (skills I had picked up in New Zealand). I was extremely well fed for these endeavours because Corry Lunn, the lady of the house, was a superb cook. She spent only minimal hours in the kitchen, however, for she had a full-time job as a clay sculptor. She made a reasonable living at her art; she lives on Vancouver Island now.

Corry's husband was building his dream home and doing car-pentry work for others. Many of the farm chores were done by visitors like myself, most of whom were only temporary. Nick

Berwian and his friend Janis were spending a year in Canada enjoying various voluntary work experiences, with an emphasis on wilderness. I asked them if they would like to help me build a cabin on a fly-in lake. They didn't have time that year, but Janis and another friend visited for a couple of weeks during the summer. That was when Janis wrote the guest book entry quoted at the beginning of this book. The young men vowed to return the following year. Nick already had building skills he had acquired in Germany, but there he had used square logs with dovetailed corners. A round-log cabin was exactly what he wanted to try.

Nick and Janis, plus Nick's girlfriend, Ellen, were flown in on a ski-equipped plane at the beginning of April while the ice was still good on my lake. We felled trees, mostly beetle-kill from a wave that had gone through in the eighties. Toboggans were placed under each end of the fallen trees, and the three harnessed themselves to ropes and dragged the logs across the ice. March, April and May are usually sunny months at Nuk Tessli and the building site welcomed the warmth. The snow began to melt and by the time the helpers left in early May, a day before the ice began to disintegrate, the foundations were in place.

Nick, Janis and other friends arrived again in the summer, although it was only Nick who stayed for the whole season. The walls and ridgepole were erected by September. Although I had so much help with this cabin, it still took most of two years to complete because I was no longer able to work on it full-time. I now had quite a few clients and other visitors to cater to. It was snowing by the time I started to build the roof, alone, in October. I managed to cover the living area before I went out for the year's book-promotion tour in mid-November. The rest of the roof was finished in March; it would be another year before the interior was completed. I moved in during the last days of 1999, ready to welcome the new millennium in what would surely be the last cabin I would ever build. Once more I lived with the debris of construction work piled up around me.

I could of course have stayed in Cabin Two, but hand-hauling firewood was such a big job I didn't want to heat two buildings.

After Nick left, I wrote letters to him about the cabin's progress. These became the framework for book number four: *Snowshoes and Spotted Dick*. (If you don't know what Spotted Dick is, I suggest you read the book to find out!) I submitted the title to the publisher without the first two words. I thought it would make everyone sit up and notice. But the publisher insisted on a bit of clarification: he thought that people might get the wrong idea.

It was Ellen, Nick's girlfriend, who told me about wwoofing. WWOOF stands for: *Willing Workers On Organic Farms* (or, more latterly, *World Wide Opportunities on Organic Farms,* as customs officials take exception to the word "work" and ban the volunteers from coming in, even though they can expect no pay). I certainly had no farm, but the organizers said it didn't matter, and soon I began to host a regular stream of people, mostly but not all young, who were happy to work for their keep in exchange for mountain experience. On the whole these people really lived up to the title of *Willing*. Some were excellent. A few were mediocre, and one or two I sent out on the next plane, but this organization has been a really great resource for me. Now there are three or four other volunteer work websites, but WWOOF was the first and was the one that made the most impact at Nuk Tessli. Not only did these volunteers bring in the firewood every year (a most time-consuming job as every piece had to be carried by foot and canoe) but they also helped clear out, and build cairns for, most of the hiking trails. For this last decade, I have rarely had to do the heaviest work alone.

I could no longer manage the four-day snowshoe treks in winter. I had to resort to flying in. But the people who put skis on their planes began to either die or move on. Visits to Nuk Tessli were by now getting much harder to arrange. The only access for me now was by helicopter. As the closest heliport was

Cabin Three.

a forty-five-minute flight away across the mountains, these trips were unbelievably spectacular, but they were also very costly. (Oddly enough, my phobia is much reduced in a helicopter and I could actually enjoy the flights. Affording them on a regular basis was not possible, though.)

Once the helicopter had taken me to Nuk Tessli, I was much more isolated than I used to be. Previously, local pilots would pop by once in a while throughout the winter with mail or fresh produce from the store. I rarely went more than three or four weeks without a visitor. Now, once the helicopter got me in there, that would be my last contact with anyone, except for an occasional radiophone conversation, for weeks. Life at Nuk Tessli was becoming much more difficult, and very much more expensive.

Spending those months at the dreary and badly insulated little cabin at Nimpo Lake would have been a nightmare for me, and

Wwoofers collecting firewood.

a new resident in the neighbourhood was making life even more unpleasant. I desperately needed an outside place of my own. All the years at Nuk Tessli had barely paid the bills, however. If I managed to get ahead by a few hundred dollars one year, the Land Office upped my expenses by thousands. I could not keep up with inflation. Thanks to the fibromyalgia, I was no longer able to tree-plant for cash. If it hadn't been for the small income I continued to receive from my writing, I would not have been able to eat.

Many times as I struggled through the wilderness with my first dog, Lonesome, I had thought about writing her story. She faithfully endured loneliness and major discomfort on my behalf. On very cold nights in the bush I would try to wrap my sleeping bag around her but she would shiver uncontrollably. I wasn't quite sure how to tackle the book at first, then I suddenly realized that she should tell the story. I had a lot of fun putting myself into her paws.

It is not considered good ethics to send a manuscript to more than one publisher at once, and they often do not look at it for a year, if at all. It was rejected in all by three publishers. "Who would want to read a book written by a dog!" one exclaimed. Consequently, it was years before the book was actually published. When *Lonesome: Memoirs of a Wilderness Dog* finally hit bookstores, it was on the bestsellers list for eighteen months, and it has far outsold any other of my books. (I am happy to say that the publisher who made the derogatory comment admits he is now kicking himself.) But unless you are a Stephen King or Michael Connelly, the fortunes of an author are meagre at best. I had a wonderful life, but the constant worry about financing it was exhausting.

In 2006, I flew in by helicopter and spent breakup at Nuk Tessli, something I had managed only twice before as I was usually away tree-planting in the spring. It was a most magical time to be there. Every day, changing ice patterns would create a new world of light and colour and sound as the ice disintegrated. It was one of the earliest springs I had experienced, and the ice went out on May 18. I could have flown to Nimpo then by plane; because Nimpo Lake goes out a month earlier, the float plane companies had already started up. But it was so beautiful, I stayed in until the middle of June. The daily record of that spring was important as I was able to round out the seasons for *A Mountain Year*, my next book. Unless they are hot topics, most books take a couple of years to go through the system, so it was a while before I saw the results. This is my favourite book. It is a hardcover; the illustrations comprise drawings and paintings of all my beloved birds and plants, and they have been reproduced in luscious colour. Thank you, Harbour Publishing, for this.

. . . .

At the beginning of 2006, I was fortunate to inherit a bit of money. I was now sixty years old. I wanted nothing more than an outside place of my own. I had planned to spend the last two weeks of June outside, partly to buy supplies for the Nuk Tessli summer season, but also to look at property. I was attracted to a derelict homestead not too far from Nuk Tessli as the float plane flies, but it was less difficult to get to as it was possible to drive in on a four-kilometre bush road. It wasn't as spectacular a place as either of my previous wilderness dwellings, needless to say, but it did have considerable privacy, great sun exposure, rugged mountain views and a capricious river known for its ability to change course with every flood. The river's headwaters were not far from Nuk Tessli, and despite the dusty road and the overgrown remnants of rotting stumps buried in the forest that indicated a history of severe logging, the water was governed by the moods of the mountains, and it sang with a wilderness song.

There was no dwelling on the property—the rancher who ran his cows there had taken down the rough cabin that had existed—and I would have to build again. However, I would have six weeks between the end of the Nuk Tessli season and the start of that fall's book tour, and being able to drive supplies to the building site would make a huge difference to the construction time. I hoped I would be able to cobble together a shelter of some sort before the winter. (I can't believe I was even thinking along those lines!)

The deposit was paid for the new property, and the Nuk Tessli food and equipment were offloaded at the float plane base. The first guests in the mountains were due to arrive in a few days, but before I went home, I treated myself to a short visit with friends. That was when I broke my leg.

The Broken Leg

The east side of the Coast Range slopes gradually; the west side plummets. Forty kilometres northwest of Nuk Tessli, however, lies an anomaly, an eight-kilometre flat, lush valley, suspended between the backbone of the Coast Range and the coast. Known as the Precipice because of the organ-pipe rimrock on one side, it is accessed by a very rough road running south from Anahim Lake. Four properties occupy the valley. The largest is a ranch; the two smaller ones at either end belong to couples who are partially self-sustaining. Dave and Rosemary Neads have inhabited the upper part of the valley for about the same length of time that I have lived in the wilderness. They built their post-and-beam house with logs they had extracted from the nearby forest using horses, and squared the timbers with a small sawmill owned by the neighbouring rancher.

The Precipice is quite a bit lower than Nuk Tessli and, although frosts are common, it is possible to grow quite a lot of produce. Rosemary maintains a garden patch and two impressive greenhouses. Most people nowadays prefer not to live by produce alone, however, and getting supplies into the Precipice requires much the same foresight as flying them into Nuk Tessli. Although it is possible to drive in and out of the Neadses' valley during summer, winter access is by snowmobile only, and there are times in the spring and fall when it is impossible to use the road at all. Like me, they must plan their shopping trips to cope with emergencies far from facilities and try to anticipate everything that might be needed for months at a time. We were naturally drawn together by our similar lifestyles—in fact, we are next-door neighbours as the plane flies, but it would not be at all practical to travel that route overland. The Neadses and I have now been friends for a great many years.

The Internet was gaining popularity and I decided it would be expedient to have a website. The only way I could receive the Internet at Nuk Tessli was via satellite, which at first was prohibitively expensive. By a quirk of fate, the Precipice had a phone line so the Neadses were already hooked up to cyberspace. Rosemary kindly offered to monitor a website for me and organize bookings, so I patched one together. Because she understood the logistics of remote living, she was one of the few people I knew who could juggle people and planes and supplies with any hope of success. I would try to remember to switch the radiophone on in the evening. If Rosemary wanted to get hold of me, she would phone somebody who had the local frequency and they would try to call in. I would then attempt to phone Rosemary directly, but if I could not get through on the Telus channel, our Nimpo contact would hold the landline receiver in one hand and the radiophone call button in the other—a somewhat cumbersome system, especially as radiophone reception was hit-and-miss, but we communicated quite successfully that way. Fortunately, Internet queries were few then: the majority of my clients were middle-aged and older, and the Internet was still a young person's game. In 2004, satellite Internet prices dropped considerably, and I was able install a system in the mountains.

I love to visit the Precipice especially in the spring, which is so far advanced, it might be on a different planet. I had missed visiting at my usual time this year as I had still been up at Nuk Tessli. After the shopping trip at the end of June, I lurched down the wet, rocky track that had been accessible only by snowmobile not too long before. Two dogs rode in the back of my van.

Raffi and Bucky were SPCA specials, both Rottweiler crosses although of very different ages and backgrounds. I confess to being lazy regarding the training I should have done, and the dogs would not readily come when called. Livestock was meant to be chased, cats were meant to be killed, gardens were meant to be dug up and peed on, other dogs were meant to be fought and traffic was something that would stop for them or drive around them. So in most circumstances, whenever I was outside, the dogs had to be kept chained and walked on leads. After two weeks on the road, both I and they were heartily sick of this treatment.

The Neadses' house perched on top of a hill overlooking a mix of trees and a small hay meadow bisected by the upper reaches of the Hotnarko River. Early in the dewy morning, before the sun had climbed over the valley's rim, I lead-walked the dogs down to the meadow. I had hoped to cross the river, but the water was still high with spring runoff and I contented myself with wading through the knee-high wet grass along the bank.

Raffi was the most biddable of the two dogs and I figured we were far enough from the Neadses' garden and cats, and the rancher's horses (the cows had already been driven up to their summer grazing), that I could let him off. He was ecstatic and he tore around in delighted circles. I needed to cross an irrigation ditch; with a jump, I could just make it over. I was in midair when Raffi's orbit connected with my trajectory—why he didn't swerve away, as he had always done before, I shall never know. His head, driven by the momentum of his forty-five kilograms, cannoned into the inside of my right knee. I fell, fortunately not into the ditch.

I picked myself up. The knee definitely had an odd, clunky feel to it, but I was able to walk slowly back up the steep trail to the house. I tied the dogs and fed them. I hobbled up the stairs to the Neadses' living area. Maybe if I sat down for a while ... but after a couple of hours I couldn't move the leg. It was not excessively sore, but it was very swollen and it simply would not bend or bear my weight.

It was Friday, July 1. There was a clinic at Anahim Lake, an hour's slow, very bumpy drive away. We phoned and spoke to one of the two nurses on duty. "I don't think we could do anything here," she said. "You are probably going to have to have an X-ray. As it's a long weekend, you'd better check to see if they have a technician on duty if you are going to Bella Coola. There'll be someone in Williams Lake, for sure."

Bella Coola was a three-and-a-half-hour drive away; Williams Lake would need at least five hours on the road. Bella Coola was a small, friendly hospital where usually everyone was treated like family. At Williams Lake, I would probably have to sit in Emergency for several hours before I would be looked at. It would be an overnight trip at least, if not two. I could not, of course, drive myself, so Rosemary would have to take me. Her health was poor and driving exacerbated her condition. Taken all around, Bella Coola was by far the preferred choice for both of us.

The following morning we left early so that we could get down the Hill and be at the hospital by 8:30 a.m. I was quite surprised to find that I was not the only battered and broken patient waiting. It happened to be the Bella Coola Rodeo weekend—of course there was an X-ray technician on duty. People who saw me there thought I had fallen off a horse.

A couple of hours later the doctor on call showed me the X-rays and pointed out the small chip that had been knocked off the inside of my tibia. It was amazing that such a little crack could cause such major incapacitation. "It's not a bad break," the doctor said cheerfully, "but you'll have to use the crutches for three months." Three months! That was the whole of the Nuk Tessli tourist season. I had clients booked to come in seven days' time and quite a busy summer spread in front of me. I had cleaned all the cabins before I had flown out, but how was I going to be able to guide people on hikes? And there was the food I would be flying into the mountains with me. How would I carry that up the steep, rocky trail from the wharf to the cabin, then up the ladder into the storage area? What was I going to do?

Some years before, a wwoofer, Hans, had come to Nuk Tessli. He was German and in his fifties already. He'd done quite a bit of livestock farming and was looking for a permanent job. He was the kind of man who could fix anything. Wwoofing was a good way for him to get about and check out the country. After his stint in the mountains with me, the rancher in the Precipice, who did not usually winter in the valley, had taken him on as a caretaker; he had lived there for two years. Now that the cows were out on their summer range, work on the ranch was at a slack period until haying started in a couple of weeks. Hans could therefore be spared to fly home with me.

I was expecting a teenaged Swiss wwoofer, Simon, in a few days, and a French couple, Estelle and Will, in about a month's time. Hans and Simon would be leaving before the French couple planned to arrive, so I wrote to them asking if they could come earlier. How fortunate I was that they were able to bring their arrival date forward; they would fly in on the same plane that would take Hans and Simon back to Nimpo. That at least would take care of all the heavy work I would have to do for the next several weeks.

Many of the clients had arranged for guided hikes, however. All four volunteers had some hiking experience, but this was in mountains with a lot of use, well-documented maps and groomed trails. Wild Canada was a whole different kettle of fish. Nuk Tessli trails don't have a great deal of traffic so only small sections are visible on the ground; they disappear where it is rocky. Hikers must follow a variety of blazes and cairns. Some consider my trails to be well marked; others get hopelessly lost. At the beginning of summer I walk the trails, cut out windfalls and re-mark stretches where blaze trees or cairns have fallen over. Before I had left for the shopping trip, there had been too much snow at higher elevations to do this.

I sat myself at Rosemary's computer and emailed all the clients. I told them I would do my best to provide a guide but could not guarantee one. Without exception everyone agreed to come anyway; if they had to find their own way about, they would manage.

I had already met one client briefly a few years before—she lives not far from Williams Lake. I knew she guided nature tours. I asked her if she could stay a bit longer and do some work for me. She replied that she would not be able to spare the time, but she had a marvellous son who would be perfect. He was twenty-nine, had guided with an outfitter since he was at high school and had also operated a sled dog tourism business. Not only was he experienced in the bush, therefore, he was also used to dealing with tourists. He was apparently between jobs right now.

He sounded too good to be true. Surely this was just a doting mother speaking. Then Dylan wrote to me—his resume was even more impressive than his mother had led me to believe. As well as his outfitting and dogsledding jobs, he'd also taken part in a Pole to Pole project while in his early twenties. Participants took a year to travel from the North Pole to South, mostly under their own power, through both the Americas, although they did fly to the Poles. Dylan had also been the stuntman in the sled dog movie *Eight Below*. I was not at all sure if this huntin', shootin', fishin', extreme dogsleddin' kind of guide would fit into gentle Nuk Tessli very well. I wrote back to him that I didn't think I could afford someone with his experience. He replied that if I could find him a couple thousand dollars for the summer, he would be happy. Any profit I might have made that year was rapidly going out the window, but this was an extremely generous offer. Dylan planned to arrive with the second batch of clients.

I didn't need a cast on my knee. The hospital had supplied a brace to keep the leg rigid, but I had been advised to fork out for a different one (more expense!) that would allow the knee to bend forward and back but not sideways. On no account was I to put weight on the leg for two months; during the third I could employ the limb cautiously but still keep using the crutches.

A couple of days later, I presented myself at the float plane base. Although Beavers are just big enough for a stretcher and are often used for medevacs, I don't suppose the pilots had flown too many people hopping around on crutches before. I wasn't even sure how I was going to be able to scale the narrow-runged ladder into the plane. But with a pull of the arms, a shuffle of the bum and a few heaves and yanks from all concerned, I was in.

The Flowerless Summer

The ground around the cabins at Nuk Tessli is lumpy and crowded with large boulders. The only flat places are the floors and the decks of the cabins. Hans's first job was to create rough rock steps between my cabin and the outhouse, a distance of about eighty metres. The steps had to be wide enough to accommodate the crutches. I was soon hopping up and down them in fine style. One of the volunteers took a picture of me swinging along. He said it looked almost like fun—which it certainly wasn't!

Hans also fixed a hand-cranked cistern pump onto the deck. I would never have been able to go down the steep trail to the lake for water, but having the pump relatively close to the cabin meant I could have access to it at any time. Of course my helpers fetched most of the water I needed, but when they were away during the day I was not totally reliant on what they brought. I still had to carry the buckets up three or four steps—clunk with the crutches, heave the bucket forward, clunk, heave, and so on. The pump was particularly useful when I wanted to do laundry.

Carrying anything was one of the more difficult tasks. A book or similar object could be moved in a supermarket shopping bag slung in one hand. But a plate of food or a drink had to be placed on a flat surface, then I would clunk forward, then the item had to be moved again and so on until it reached its destination. Fortunately, the cabin was not very big. Chores like sweeping the

Me on crutches at Nuk Tessli.

floor were a real pain. Clunk, sweep. Clunk, sweep. It was difficult to get into the corners or under seats with the broom. When Estelle and Will arrived, the first thing Estelle asked for was a cloth and warm soapy water to wash down the out-houses. I apologized for their state—it is not a job I usually expect wwoofers to do. "Simon and Hans tried their best," I said. "Oh," Estelle said dismissively with a wonderfully Gallic shrug, "Zey are boys! Zey are boys!"

The first clients were a doctor and his wife. He was so tickled at the idea of me being at Nuk Tessli on crutches, he wrote a story about it for a medical journal. Poor things, they tried to guide themselves but came to grief on the trails. They took it all with good humour, though.

Dylan arrived with the next batch of visitors. I welcomed them on the wharf, directing the clients to their cabins and promising them tea or coffee in Cabin Three as soon as they were ready. I told them to make themselves at home if they got there before I did, as I would take a little time hopping my way up the rock steps.

Dylan is extremely tall. His hair was pulled into a ponytail and a baseball cap was yanked low on his face. He barely spoke to me when he arrived, but headed up the trail and when I arrived at my cabin he was already pouring coffee into the clients' mugs. He had seamlessly taken charge. I was to find that his mother had not been accurate in her praise of him—he was even better than she had said. He was quiet, and very welcoming and popular with the tourists. Even though the country was all new to him, he understood it perfectly. As well as taking the guests out, he also accompanied the wwoofers on firewood expeditions, on which he did the chainsaw work, and hikes to brush out trails or rebuild cairns when needed.

And so it was that, after its dramatic beginning, that summer at Nuk Tessli was destined to run smoothly. It was an odd situation for me, however. *This*, I thought, *is what it's like to be a housewife.* I felt quite left out. Dylan and the visitors would be chatting away about their adventures of the day; I was simply the person who provided the food. It was not intentional on their behalf, of course, but it made me realize how much I enjoyed being the centre of attention in my Queendom. The wwoofers, Dylan and the paying guests would set off gaily each morning, and I was left with the dishes. It was a glorious summer weatherwise, the best I remember at Nuk Tessli. Lots of sunshine but never too hot, and the bugs were therefore less onerous than usual. As the main flower season approached, I found it hard not to be despondent. "Don't worry," the visitors would say. "We'll take lots of pictures and show you." But that just made it worse.

Estelle and Will had spent several winters working in a major ski resort in the French Alps. Estelle was the receptionist for the resort's spa, and Will worked in a sports store. Their summers were taken up with travelling. Estelle was the epitome of Frenchness: attractive, vivacious and with an accent like Maurice Chevalier. Her English was good, but she never once got her h's in the right place. If one was required, she would miss it out. If a word started with a vowel, she would add an *h*. She always went to the "hout-'ouse," and I call it that to this day.

Estelle was a good cook, Will not too bad and Dylan could put together a decent enough meal when required. I didn't expect them to prepare food when they were busy all day, but it was nice to have something different once in a while. Will's grandmother was Ukrainian and one day, under his guidance, we made perogies from scratch. We produced about two dozen and it took forever. He told me that his grandmother was an expert at these: for her own eightieth birthday party she had made five hundred.

At Nuk Tessli the only means of cooking is with wood. All the cabins are equipped with heater stoves and food is prepared on top. The only oven is a big heap of rocks with a hole in it large enough to accommodate a couple of big loaves of bread. This oven took about three hours of hot fires to heat, then the ashes were raked out and the bread thrown free-form onto the hot stones. It took such a lot of wood to make the oven hot enough, it made sense to bake all day, and I usually produced several batches of bread, a heavy trail mix cake or two and maybe a pizza or baked potatoes at the end. The French couple made some excellent pizzas.

. . . .

Early during my time at Nuk Tessli, a bear broke into my cabins on more than one occasion. The trappers were operating then and they used to leave skinned carcasses around their own shelters. Rotten meat is a bruin's favourite food, and these titbits were a delectable spring feast for a bear just out of bed. The animals soon learned that cabins meant food, and my place became another pit stop en route. Twice I came back from tree-planting season to find windows broken, stovepipes bashed apart allowing the soot to get everywhere, and books and utensils bearing the evidence of tooth and claw. On one occasion I was greeted by barn swallows flying in and out of the broken window. They had built a nest among some books on a shelf above my bed. It would have been an interesting project to let them be, but the bugs were too bad to leave the window without screens.

I waged war on this bear, trying to set up a shotgun trap at the window so that if he attempted to get in again, he would shoot himself. Whenever I arrived back at the cabin after a hike or a day of working on the trail, I would approach with great trepidation, bear spray at the ready, in case a bruin was badly injured and draped in a bloody mass over the windowsill. But it

Baking day—loaves and pizzas made in the outdoor stone oven.

never happened. When the gun was there, the cabin was inviolate; if I did not set up the trap, he would be in again.

A year or two later, I found the remains of a bear carcass very close to where I had pitched my tent while building Cabin One. Wolves had eaten most of the carcass—a lot of scat full of bone chips lay around—but the skull was unharmed close by. It stank of putrefaction, but I was not going to let this treasure go to waste. The ground was too rocky to bury it and let soil organisms do the cleaning, so I put the head in an old bucket and boiled and scraped and boiled and scraped, and finally tied the skull high on the ridge of a roof out of the way of the dogs and other bears, hoping the birds would pick it clean. Bear experts have seen this skull and no one can decide if it is a record-sized black bear or a medium grizzly. The bear that I had seen by the cabins several times while I was having trouble was a fine-looking male black bear, and during the previous winter, the dogs had dug up part of a foot with three remaining claws not far from where I later found the carcass. These were large but definitely black bear claws; remains of two bear carcasses at the same place would be very unlikely. Whether or not this animal was my antagonist I will never know. At the same time the trappers had stopped operating this far back into the bush so there were now no spring goodies for the bears to feast on. Whatever the reason, I have never had a cabin break-in since.

It is common sense to keep any bear's temptation to the minimum. They will eat anything, and they love human food, rotten or otherwise. Before I went into the bush I had often read about trappers' caches. They would lop three or four trees off about five metres high and build a small log shed on these pillars to house their provisions. The ladder that was used to reach the cache was taken down when the trappers were not at home. These stores were often broken into nonetheless. I didn't want to build this kind of structure, but figured that the attics of my buildings would do well enough. Unlike most bush cabins, the roofs at Nuk Tessli are all metal and built steeply to shed the sometimes heavy snow. Not only are they difficult to walk on, they also make quite a lot of storage space underneath. I constructed permanent ladders or steps in the porches to reach these attics and blocked the top of the steps with heavy trap doors. I figured I would never be able to keep a determined bear from breaking in downstairs, because he would be able to stand on the ground and rip things apart with the full power of his body. But if he shinnied up to the gable end, whatever damage he tried to do there would have to be with one paw only as he would be hanging on with the other three. And in fact my attics have all been inviolate.

I buy most of Nuk Tessli's supplies in bulk at the beginning of summer: eight sixteen-kilogram bags of dog food, five twenty-kilogram bags of flour, five kilograms of salt, five kilograms of peanut butter and so on. There was no room to store this stuff downstairs, and the steps into the attic were so narrow it was impossible to use the crutches to get up them. Bum-shuffling was tedious in the extreme so I would send my helpers up for a handful of this or a pinch of that. There were some puzzling results for some of our earlier meals. The problem, we finally realized, was in the definition of a handful. Dylan's huge paws were the size of a dinner plate; Estelle's dainty fingers barely spanned a saucer. My hands were somewhere in between.

. . . .

Although hiking was out of bounds for me, it didn't stop me from paddling a canoe. I had five craft of various proportions, all flown in at different times strapped to the floats of a plane. The biggest was dubbed the barge because it was used to carry loads that were heavy or poorly balanced, like firewood and beginner canoeists. If someone held this canoe very firmly at the wharf, I could lower myself into it. By tying it in a certain way and shuffling onto my bum, I could get out unaided, although I had to leave the boat fastened to the wharf. Often on those lovely summer mornings, I would ask someone to load me up before they took off for the day, and I would spend a couple of hours paddling about. Usually I would have a go at fishing. There are countless pan-sized rainbow trout in the lake. Before that summer I never spent a lot of time trying to catch them: I was too busy, the wind was often too strong and if I wanted to relax, I preferred to read a book. That year, however, I returned home several times with a good supper for us all.

I know very little about fishing and my equipment is far from sophisticated, being a line wound around a tin can. I found it much easier to get a fish into the boat with the can; I never really got the hang of a rod. I would unroll the line and drag a hook far behind the canoe. If I felt something on the line, I would yank it in fast. If the fish did not land in the big basin I kept in the bottom of the boat and flopped on the line, I would sometimes end up with interesting tangles, but mostly I could pay the filament out again without problem. These fishing forays had the added bonus of being the only way I could see something different from the views from the cabins' decks.

Once, when the lake was mirror calm, I was entertained by three ospreys. They skimmed over the water and plunged for a fish, breaking the glassy surface into shards. They oriented their catch with its head pointing forward (as opposed to eagles, who carry their fish crossways) and flew to a perch to enjoy their lunch. Another time, when I was paddling slowly near the eagles' nest at the head of the lake, a parent bird seemed about to launch itself after a fish I had on the line. I yelled and waved my paddle. Not that I cared about the eagle taking the fish, but I didn't want it to give a fish with a hook in it to its young. The eagle took off and swooped low over the water where the fish had been, but because I had stopped paddling, it had sunk beyond the eagle's reach.

Another project I tackled that summer was spinning enough wool for a sweater. My mother had been a compulsive knitter and she taught me how to do it when I was a child. I learned to spin in New Zealand and loved the idea of being able to cut the raw fleece off a sheep and produce a finished garment. For a lot of my early years in Canada I did a great deal of spinning, dyeing the wool with plants and weaving garments for sale. In truth, however, I found spinning to be just as tedious as knitting and, since I had started writing, rarely did either anymore. However, I had some rather nice fleece and figured that I could make use of my sedentary hours and also get a bit of exercise.

Always fascinated by craft techniques, once I had mastered the wheel, I picked up the art of creating a thread with a spindle. This is simply a stick with a round weight or disc near the bottom; an easy way to make one is to use a pencil and a slice of potato. The device is whirled like a top and the teased thread is fed into it until a length is spun; the result is then wound onto the spindle. West Coast First Nations people used a large spindle whose point rested on the ground. The stem was twirled against their thighs. In South America, however, the spindles are small and either allowed to drop through the air or spun in a bowl. It was a common sight to see both women and men performing this task while either shepherding sheep or sitting on a bus.

Spindles were for sale in the markets; many tourists bought them but I never saw one who could handle them. Already experienced at this, I lost no time in picking up a spindle and some alpaca fleece. It turned out to be a great way to make friends! The local women were always surprised that I could do this, and even approved of the quality of the thread I was producing, although I could never master their dexterity. My Spanish was not good but I tried to explain that I learned how to do it in New Zealand, and that usually I used *la rueca*, the spinning wheel. "Oh," was the inevitable comment. "You mean machine spinning!"

Well, machine spinning was what I was going to do at Nuk Tessli. At first I used the treadle with my good leg, then with both legs. I am sure that the pumping exercise was perfect for my knee. I ended the summer with a ton of spun wool (some of which I dyed with onion skins) but, years later, I have never got around to knitting the planned sweater with it.

Late in the summer, Dylan planned to guide a small party up through the second lake, after which they would walk up the trail I had made to a third, which was the lake I had first encountered after initially hiking up from the trench. I called it Boundary Lake as the Tweedsmuir Park boundary twisted around it.

Getting in and out of a canoe at either end of the portage was quite a bit more challenging than at the wharf, and it took me a while to crutch-hop over all the cross-logs, but Dylan held the boat firm and made the trip possible for me. I couldn't do the hike, but getting into the upper lake for a change of scenery was a real treat.

September was already well along and it was time to leave for my new winter place on the Chilcotin. I took the longest walk of the season, about half a kilometre round the tussocky meadow behind Cabin One. Swampy in the spring, it was dry at this time of year. The knee brace kept sliding down my leg. The flowers had finished and fall colours were already spangling the bushes and the small plants between the frost-browned sedges. The dark purple leaves of the mountain daisy; the soft salmon jewels of the northern starflower; the ruby leaves of the dwarf birch. What a waste of a season for me. But how lucky I had been to have such good helpers. Without them I would never have been able to stay at Nuk Tessli at all.

The Big Snow

With excellent volunteer help I had managed to erect the shell of a cabin in the fall, and after I came back from my book tour I went through the dreadful but very familiar process of building a cabin while I was living in it.

Ginty Creek is in a comparatively dry area. Knee-deep snow is common; sometimes there is not enough to warrant having the road ploughed. But the winter of 2006–7 presented us with a very heavy snowfall. About half a metre came down before Christmas, and two other major falls dumped in January. The pack was chest deep. As I was the one who maintained the four kilometres of road that joined me to Highway 20, organizing snowploughs became a new chore for me. It was part, I suppose, of the process of becoming more "civilized."

The first of several groups of wwoofers arrived in mid-April the following year. We put a roof on the cabin's porch, cut out a road to a site at the other end of the property, and started to clear the area where I would build my dream home. The last three volunteers, two young men from Belgium and a woman from Switzerland, worked extremely hard for me at Ginty Creek and were promised time at Nuk Tessli as a reward.

When I tree-planted for a living, I would stay with the crew through the busiest of the season, which finished at the end of June or in early July. With a few thousand more dollars in the bank to pay for Nuk Tessli's supplies, I would hike over the mountains to the cabins. There was usually a lot of snow at high elevations at that time, but most of it was firm. In the latter parts of the day, especially if it was sunny, the top few centimetres would become slushy, which slowed me down quite a bit, but I never sank very far. Sometimes I had problems crossing creeks, which were roaring with snowmelt at that time, but if I was lucky there might still be a snow bridge spanning the current. It was generally precarious and I didn't always make it over without falling in, but my boots got pretty sodden anyway trudging through all those kilometres of thawing snow.

Once tree-planting was no longer possible for me, I could return to Nuk Tessli almost a month earlier as that was when the ice went out of the lake and my supplies could be flown in. However, when I first tried to hike home in early June, I was turned back well before the treeline. If I could have reached the alpine I probably would have been all right, but there was still a lot of snow in the forest on the north side of Halfway Mountain, and this was waist deep and rotten. I struggled for a while, but my dogs couldn't handle it either, and we were getting nowhere. So, despite my flying phobia I psyched myself up to get into those pitiful little dragonflies and endure the twenty minutes of hell. The euphoria once I got my feet back on the ground was so incredible that it was almost worth going through the agony beforehand.

Over the years, the average time for breakup at Nuk Tessli had proved to be late May or early June. I had twice recorded an open lake in the middle of May, and the latest I'd had to wait so far was June 4. Because of the excessive snow, 2007 was obviously going to be a late spring. Nimpo Lake goes out approximately a month before Nuk Tessli, and whatever float plane companies are operating establish themselves soon afterwards. I always ask local pilots, private or otherwise, to give me a progress report as to what is going on in the mountains, should they be flying in that direction.

There have been as many as three float plane companies based at Nimpo, but Tweedsmuir Air, operating out of Stewart's Lodge, was the only outfit in business that year. Most of their flights were to resorts north of the highway, but the lodge had two cabins not many air kilometres from Nuk Tessli. They would need to go up there to spring clean them. These cabins were on lower lakes but it wouldn't be very far out of their way to swing over Nuk Tessli. Tweedsmuir Air also ran flightseeing tours. The plane would cross the trench near Lonesome Lake, waltz around the massive drop of Hunlen Falls, then do a loop over several glaciers before coming back over the trench again. As they flew to Nimpo from there, they would pass directly over my lake.

Duncan Stewart, the owner of Tweedsmuir Air, phoned on June 4 to tell me that the ice was still on the lake but it was very broken. He figured it would go out in a day or two. I booked two flights for the seventh: a Beaver to transport me, a big chunk of supplies and the dogs, and a Cessna 185 to take in the three wwoofers. Because they had worked so well for me at Ginty Creek, I splurged the extra hundred dollars on top of the normal flight price so they could have a flightseeing tour. They would take off first; we would give them a half hour or so and they would be waiting for me on Nuk Tessli's wharf to help unload the Beaver when we arrived.

We taxied out into the lake about an hour after the Cessna had taken off. But the pilot, who was listening to radio communications on his earphones, turned to me and said, "Here's the 185 coming back. Your passengers are still on board. They couldn't land. Your lake is still frozen." This was undoubtedly a new record for lateness. It was in fact the twelfth before we could fly in. Remnants of ice hung around in one of the bays for quite a few more days after we had arrived.

Normally, when I reach Nuk Tessli at the beginning of summer, all the snow has gone from around the buildings. A few drifts always linger by my old campsite, which is where the wind piles them, but this year, there was snow everywhere. An enormous chunk covered the trail up to Cabin Three. We had to cut ice steps in it so we could carry up the freight that was to be stored in the attic.

Boris, one of the young Belgians, was an experienced canoeist. His grandfather had a farm by the sea and Boris often took a boat out into the waves. One evening, after I had gone to bed, he and the other young man, Sven, decided to go onto the water. They didn't ask me first; I would certainly have dissuaded them. It would have seemed calm enough beside the wharf but farther out there were whitecaps on the water, a sign that it was pretty windy away from the shelter of the land.

An experienced canoeist Boris might have been, but he was only eighteen and not very good at judging safety for others. He took the big, heavy canoe I call the barge: it is almost impossible to tip it over. He certainly made a wise choice for himself. Sven, however, was very green on the water. He chose the smallest canoe. It had hardly any freeboard and was useful only for playing around the dock. Sven was very tall. He did not know that kneeling would give him more control and he sat with his knees almost up to his chin. (I saw photographs.) Of course, as soon as he drew away from the wharf, the wind and waves caught him broadside and over he went. Ice still lay in places on the lake so the water must have been pretty cold. Boris paddled back to try to rescue him. Sven managed to tip him over as well. Fortunately, they had at least had enough sense to wear life jackets.

They were about a hundred metres out and were able to swim to the shore, dragging one of the upturned boats with them. Monika, the Swiss woman, had observed all this from Cabin Two, which the volunteers were using. She had no experience at all with boats so wisely did not try to go out to them. She at once booted up the fire and started to heat water; by the time the young men reached the cabin—shivering almost uncontrollably—she was able to warm them up. They then went together in the canoe they had brought in with them and fetched the other, which by then had been blown quite a long way down the lake.

I didn't find out about all this until the following morning. "Why didn't you come and get me?" I said. "We thought you'd be mad," they replied. Well, I probably would have been, but as long as they were both safe, that was the main thing. There were consequences for Sven, however. He lost his camera, which was a disappointment, but he also developed a bad ear infection. He had left home with a hole in his eardrum. There had been no time to have the required operation before he wanted to leave for Canada so, with strict warnings to keep his ear dry, he started his vacation. Within a couple of days of his dunking, the ear was painful and weeping pus. He flew out and took a plane to Vancouver where he sought medical help. He was told he should go back to his doctor in Belgium; thus ended his Canadian summer.

He later wrote to me wondering if anyone could rescue his camera. He knew the camera itself would be useless, but the memory card might still function and it held irreplaceable pictures—Sven was an excellent photographer. He could describe almost exactly the place where he had tipped over. A few years earlier, however, a fisheries survey had been executed at the lake. As well as trapping and counting fish, the technicians had measured the depth and temperature of the water. Where Sven lost his camera, the lake was comparatively shallow, being only twenty metres deep. (It is sixty metres deep in the widest spot.) But the records showed all the bottom of the lake to be dead flat. The signals were unable to penetrate the layer of organic sludge that carpeted the floor of the lake. Being so flat over such a large area indicated that the sludge was very deep. No one would have wanted to dive down twenty metres in that cold water anyway, but it would have made no difference if they did: that camera would have been instantly swallowed by the sludge and gone forever.

The cold and lack of oxygen would preserve the camera well, though. One imagines aliens walking over the earth, long after it has dried up. As they kick up the dust in the bottom of what once had been my lake, maybe they will stumble over the camera. Perhaps they will be able to retrieve the pictures and see what the earth looked like way back when.

. . . .

When the cost for satellite Internet came down, I decided it was something I had to have, and I forked out for a technician to come and set it up for me. Not only did I have to pay for the equipment and the installation fee, I also had to cover the costs of the technician's four-hour-each-way road time—and of course his flights. How wonderful, though, to have this service, especially as phone contact was so erratic. In the early months of 2006, some technical glitch happened and the satellite arm had to be adjusted. It took me all day climbing up the ladder to turn the arm a fraction, then down the ladder to check the computer, repeating this every five minutes, but I was able to do the job myself. Now, however, the Internet provider had switched to a new satellite. The old dish and arm no longer worked at all. One of the things I had bought on that year's pre-season shopping trip was a new set of equipment.

Boris and Sven took down the old dish and set up the new one. I was aware that the angle of the arm had to be quite a bit different, but try as we might, we could not get it to pick up a signal. I had bought a satellite finder, but it was not accurate enough: the adjustments of this new equipment seemed to be much more delicate. I was able to get through on the radiophone to Rosemary at the Precipice and ask her to arrange for a technician to come in. I had explained the situation to her before I had left Ginty Creek; if radiophone reception was poor, she would still know, by the very fact that I was trying to phone her, that a technician was required. If we had been able to install the arm ourselves, she would have received an email.

Ever mindful of *nuk tessli*'s powerful forces, I had mounted the dishes on the sheltered end of the cabin. The tech had a gizmo

The Lookout above Nuk Tessli.

and he found the correct angle, but he said that he could not receive a signal because a tree was in the way. It was a magnificent tree and I didn't want to take it down. He said the alternative was to put the dish on the other end of the building. I worried about the hurricane blasts that frequently hit that end of the cabin. The tech seemed to think it would be okay, but most people have no idea what these mountain winds can be like. I bowed to his expertise and the tech mounted everything, plugged in his box of tricks and was connected. Eight years later, it is still there and working fine. I can only assume it has survived because the dish is edge-on to the worst of the winds; I'm sure if it had been facing them it would have been ripped away.

. . . .

One of the first chores when getting back to Nuk Tessli in the spring is to check on the trails to see what maintenance they might need. The three wwoofers and I armed ourselves with a

Meadow behind the Lookout.

bowsaw and axe and set off on a hike to the Lookout.

We left early so that we could climb on the frost; otherwise the snow in the bush would have been too soft. It would thaw before we came down, but then we would not be fighting gravity. The weather was cool and windless, but humid and somewhat thundery. This produced a silvery grey light. In the basin behind the Lookout, the snow and occasional pieces of half-thawed water with its blue, submerged ice made for some dramatic effects. The hike was fun, but trail work was impossible as all the cairns were buried.

As always after a winter of heavy snow, there were dire predictions of flooding should there be a heat wave. But in my experience, big-snow winters produce cool, wet summers. This year was no exception. With all that melting snow, the lake was about as full as it ever gets and it stayed high for a long time.

Pine branches can stand a few days' submersion but this year, those that hung into the lake were drowned too long, and when the water finally receded, a line of twigs covered in dead needles marked the highest level of the water.

Usually, in a late, cool spring, the bugs don't become a problem until early July. But they thrive in a high-water year, and they were terrible the moment we arrived. Mosquitos lay their eggs just above the waterline; by the time they breed, the water level has dropped from its peak. The eggs don't hatch until they are covered with water again. They can survive in the earth for many years. Consequently, excessive high water causes many generations' eggs to hatch. Mosquitos are also more active in dull, humid weather, and we had more than enough of that. Blackflies hatch in fast-moving streams. The larvae snaffle food as it whirls by them while they cling to underwater stones.

The alpine meadows responded well to all that moisture, though. In a dry year, the blooming times of plants are staggered and earlier species dry up fast. In a late, wet year, everything flowers at once. On August 4 I had a rare day alone, and I treated myself to a day hike into the Mammary Meadows. For several hours I wallowed in a spectacular display of blue lupins, red paintbrush, yellow arnica and senecio, white valerian and a host of other smaller blossoms. I wore a headnet, and homemade mosquito screen gloves on my hands, and have never been so badly bitten in my life. I have a picture of one of the dogs looking cute in the flowers while around his head are swirling about two hundred blackflies.

I had owned Raffi and Bucky for a few years by now. Raffi had a gentle nature on the whole, but Bucky never got over the aggressiveness that he brought with him when I picked him up from the SPCA. He killed any creature he could get hold of. He couldn't run very fast, but he could snatch a bird out of the air as it whizzed by his nose. For many years I have kept bird records for various groups. If a dead bird was found, I was supposed to note the reason for its demise. All too often I would have to write, "Dog ate it."

Later in the year I started another hike toward the Mammaries. Not too far from the cabin, the trail climbs beside a creek. Sometimes the vegetation is quite thick along there. In a patch of subalpine fir and willow brush, a large animal suddenly crashed across the creek. I didn't see it and could only guess as to what it was. The dogs took off. Even Raffi wouldn't come back when called under those circumstances. The dogs didn't cross the creek to follow the large animal, however. I could hear Bucky's excited yap going up the trail on my side of the stream, and then I heard it coming back toward me. Suddenly, within arm's reach, a pony-sized moose calf galloped by. I stepped off the trail. I could have touched it. It was bawling for its mother, a high calf-like *meh*, and I was pretty scared that the mother moose would attack as they can be very aggressive when their young are threatened. But Mum had disappeared.

This was all happening very quickly. I was yelling at the dogs, of course. I even whacked Bucky with a walking pole as he flew by, but he never missed a stride. Raffi tore after him; he faltered briefly at my voice, but the thrill of the chase was too much for him. All three animals disappeared downstream and I could soon no longer hear them.

Usually when the dogs chased something they soon ran out of steam. I could expect them to find me again a few minutes later. Alternatively, they would go home. They knew the way up the Mammaries, and I continued along the trail.

Friends were staying at Nuk Tessli: Paul vanPeenen, his wife, Janice Ebenstiner, and two others. They were due to fly out to Nimpo late in the morning; sure enough, while I was plodding up Long Meadow, I heard the plane taking off. They land quietly, but the power needed for takeoff produces a huge bellow that can be heard over any wind or water noise.

I remained dogless for the rest of the day and enjoyed my hike along the North Ridge. Raffi and Bucky were waiting by the cabins when I arrived home some hours later. On the table was a note from Paul.

> *The dogs killed something way across the lake. We don't know what they were chasing—looked like a moose calf—but it got into the water and the dogs swam after it. It almost got to the other side and then just seemed to give up. The dogs lost interest then and swam home.*

This, as far as I was concerned, was the last straw. Bucky was probably about seven years old by then. Friends who lived close to the SPCA where Bucky came from arrived at Nuk Tessli later that summer. I asked them to take the dog back and return him to the SPCA. The husband took pity on him, and my friends kindly kept the dog themselves until he died. He was given an active life: my friends are runners, cyclists, skiers and so on. But Bucky spent the rest of his life on a lead.

Bucky's new family was visiting Nuk Tessli because I threw a party. It was my birthday; I was sixty years old. I had hosted a couple of other parties at Nuk Tessli, one for my fiftieth birthday and one for Cabin Three's housewarming. Some people hiked in, others flew. On the occasions that we sat inside, the cabin was bursting at the seams. Cousins came from Germany, and my brother flew over from England. I had not seen him for thirty years. My mother, until shortly before her death, had kept us in touch with each other. We had not had a lot of direct contact since our mid-teens, although Michael had meticulously handled all the paperwork involved with our mother's death.

Michael is a clever man who can do many different things. Considered a dunce at school, where he failed everything including woodwork, as soon as he got into the world, he blossomed. He now owns and runs the family business of furniture making. In his spare time he acquired a degree in geology through the Open University. Courses used to be offered by mail and are now completed through the Internet. Michael teaches geology and planetary science for the same institution. Despite our varied successes in life, it was interesting to see how we immediately fell into the kind of verbal scrapping that we had perfected in our childhood!

Tweedsmuir Air ferried people back and forth, and when Duncan Stewart himself brought in a planeload, he said I was exactly as old as the Beaver. The aircraft had first been flown on August 16, 1947, which was the day I had advertised for the party. In fact, my actual birthday had been a few days before, but I had been busy with clients then. Manufacture of the plane had ceased in 1967, but it was still considered the most useful aircraft in this part of the world because of the altitude and size of the lakes. The Beaver has the shortest takeoff requirements in proportion to the load it can carry of any of the small aircraft. It doesn't climb very quickly, though, and pilots prefer lakes to be open-ended—that is, to have mountain walls on only two sides.

The original Beaver that Duncan bought was built in 1949 and has the most flying hours of any Beaver in the world. He bought another in 1996 that had been launched in 1953. The motors are of course rigorously overhauled, as are the floats, but these aircraft were built to last. Duncan had recently installed a new dashboard into the older Beaver. He reinstated the original-style flight instruments, but I felt that the panel into which they were set should have been kept for historic reasons. Sure, it was looking a bit scuffed and weathered, but the plane had originally been used for training war personnel, and the old dash had featured a little lever on the passenger side. It looked just like an old-fashioned light switch. It was labelled "bomb dump."

Pandemonium Pass

A s you look up the lake from the cabins at Nuk Tessli, it seems as though you can simply canoe to the end of the water, then start climbing the snow-covered mountains that lie there. Inexperienced people often assume that the glaciers can be reached in half a day. In fact these mountains are a considerable distance from Nuk Tessli, and are divided from it by the great north–south trench.

At first, I thought there were two mountains visible through the window. Monarch, on the left, is much higher than Migma on the right, but because Monarch is much farther away, the two look much the same size. When I acquired maps of the area, I realized that there are in fact three mountains in this group. The long skyline ridge that I thought was attached to Monarch is separated by glaciers, and is named Concubine Peaks. Most of the lower peaks around Nuk Tessli remain anonymous as they are not challenging enough to attract serious climbers. It is the bigger mountains that have the cachet, and their fanciful names were invented by the original conquerors. (In front of Monarch is a much smaller peak named the Queen. Obviously, all these climbers were male.)

The Concubine ridge is saw-toothed, and it must be knife-edged at its lowest part, for even with the naked eye, it is possible to see a couple of stacks. These are pillars of rock that break off from the main mass in unstable terrain. I have no idea of the size

View through Nuk Tessli's window.

of these stacks; it is difficult to determine from so far away, but their vertical walls glow red in the early morning sun. They are not marked on any map; most local topography was deduced from aerial photos and such details were not recorded. With the aid of binoculars or a good Zoom lens, a third stack is seen. It is to the left of the others, and is as fine as a needle. Climbers sometimes tackle Monarch (which is quite a technical ascent) but I have never heard of anyone referring to these stacks.

Two major creeks fall into the trench from this mountain complex. Pandemonium Creek cascades down the north edge of Migma, and Success Creek flows between Migma and Monarch. The latter's headwaters are among the glaciers tumbling from the Concubine ridge. Near the treeline are two small lakes, both known as Success Lakes (somebody must have had a satisfying ascent). The lower Success Lake is just big enough to land a Beaver on and this is where many aspiring climbers are dropped. The Beaver can't take off loaded so all hikers must either scramble down the rough and bluffy creek to get to Knot Lake in the bottom of the trench, or head east and walk for four or five days to reach Hunlen Falls and the tourist trail out to the road. I had hiked most of that route when I still lived at Lonesome Lake. A friend and I backpacked up the old surveyor's trail to the lake chain that feeds Hunlen Falls, then scrambled to the treeline and managed to walk around the mountains more or less at that altitude until we reached Pandemonium Pass. It didn't look very far from there to the upper Success Lake. We could see part of a high shelf that covered most of the distance; it appeared to be no more difficult than the country we had so far been hiking through. We had no time to go farther, however.

One little treat was to find a small clump of penstemon, of a species I had not seen before. Its two-centimetre-long purple trumpet flowers were clumped around a small cushion of miniscule leaves. I knew very little about alpine plants at that time. Later, while exploring Nuk Tessli's environs, I occasionally came across similar flowers, which I was able to identify as Davidson's penstemon. I often wondered if the penstemon I had found at Pandemonium Pass was the same species. I remember plants without any conscious effort. They are what I use as signposts to find my way around cities. In November and December, which are the usual months when I go to Vancouver for book tours, I would be lost without the beds of pansies and frilly ornamental cabbages, or the oddly shaped pruned city trees.

About eight years after I arrived at Nuk Tessli, I thought I would climb up Pandemonium Creek to the pass and see if I could find the penstemon again. The route that would take me to the bottom of the trench would, for part of the way, retrace my steps to Lonesome Lake. The tricky bit would be to connect with the start of the game trail at the top of the bluffs. There was a lot of bush to bash through before I got there, and I had no idea if I would be able to find it. Without it, I would be unable to negotiate the cliffs and reach the bottom.

It was early August and gloriously hot, still weather. I hiked up past Boundary Lake, crossed the invisible edge into Tweedsmuir Provincial Park, then dropped, gradually at first, through the thick slide alder and misery bush. The latter is also known as stinking azalea, and my hands soon reeked of skunk. After some hours, I reached the steep bit. Being much lower in altitude, most of the forest there was fir, and I needed to find a room-sized stand of pines that had died in the 1980s wave of beetle-kill. I made a few errors and found myself either dropping into a vertical-sided creek or hung up on bluffs, neither of which I was going to be able to handle. It was hard to remember exactly what the trees had looked like; besides, they had been dead then and it was likely that many of them would no longer be standing.

Then I found a rocky knoll where a bunch of dead pines had fallen over. They had made a huge tangle and many were too high for me to step over and too low to crawl under. A real mess to negotiate, especially with a pack on. My dogs, Sport and Lonesome, were often unable to squeeze through and I had to keep taking their loads off. But in every tiny piece of ground between the fallen trunks, there were deer, moose, goat, wolf and bear prints and droppings. Despite the obstacles it was still the only way down into the valley. There was not much wear on the ground at first, but when I found moose poop on some steep rock steps, I knew I must on the right track. Soon I connected with the deep game trail that had been worn into the duff, and from there the descent was easy. I was pretty thirsty by that point, but the creek that I was loosely following was at the bottom of a very steep gully into which I couldn't climb. As soon as the ground levelled out enough for me to reach water, which was pretty much at the bottom of the trench, I gratefully made camp.

Now I was faced with the swamp. I remembered the difficult time I had experienced when I had come up from Lonesome Lake. From the top of the steep bit I had occasional glimpses of the area, and at its southern end, which is where Pandemonium Creek entered the valley, it was narrower and also contained a big chunk of mature conifers. Conifers would likely mean drier ground.

Many game paths contour the valley through the comparatively open forest just where it starts to slope up the side. It was only up and down trails that were scarce. I soon found one of these and walked in the direction of Pandemonium Creek. There was much evidence of animal traffic down there. On every little gravel bar beside a creek fresh grizzly tracks were imprinted. At one point, I encountered a moose with two well-grown calves. Her eyes bugged out—it is an amazing look!—and I thought she was going to charge, but she decided to follow her calves and beat a retreat instead. The tall coastal forest hid much of the view, but I walked until I judged myself opposite Pandemonium Creek. I couldn't avoid the swamp altogether, but it was mercifully short, and soon I found myself hopping over boulders, some half overgrown and some still recently scoured with water.

Pandemonium Creek had been dammed, probably by a slide of either rock or ice, in heavy fall rains in 1937. When the water had piled up enough, the dam collapsed and the creek blew out with such force that metre-thick cedars were sliced off right across the valley. The creek had changed course in that flood; instead of flowing south into Knot Lake, it now delivered its glacial silt into the Atnarko. The Atnarko had been, until then, a clear-water stream and was a major salmon spawning ground. Fisheries maintained that glacial silt would smother the eggs and seriously damage the salmon stock, although many rivers salmon travel up are full of glacial silt and I am not sure why this would create a problem in one river but not another. A crew was sent in there to divert the creek back into Knot Lake. Jack Turner, Trudy's husband, had been hired to cut a trail along the valley from their place, and they must have got horses in there somehow as to my immense surprise, in this wildest of wild country, I found a big abandoned stone-boat and a few half-buried steel cables.

I had chosen early August for this trip as that would likely be the best time to see the greatest number of flower species, even though some of the early ones might be past their best. I also figured that the creeks would have reduced quite a bit in size, but Pandemonium Creek was still roaring, no doubt because of its glacial origins. Where it erupted from the valley side, vertical cutbanks twenty metres high reared above the water. The glacial gravel and boulders that they were composed of were so precariously balanced, it seemed as though a puff of wind would bring them avalanching down. The shattered trunks and roots of ruined trees still spiked the tops of these cliffs. I had once met hikers who had found their way down Pandemonium Creek so I began to climb fairly confidently. But I realized later that the hikers had come down in September: probably the water had been lower then. The narrow gravel bar I started on was soon cut off by the creek as it slammed into my side of the canyon. Another gravel bar had appeared on the far side by this time, but the wild, opaque water was impossible to cross. I scrambled up the loose cutbanks a bit but soon ran into country that was far too steep and precarious for me. I had to abandon my hopes of reaching Pandemonium Pass from that direction.

With several days' food and glorious weather, I thought I would try to get to Knot Lake. Once Pandemonium Creek reached the swamp, it spread into several skeins and, although they were not easy to cross, I was able to do so and eventually reached the lake shore. The stand of conifers I had observed from the top of the steep bit proved to be old-growth cedar. The trees were tucked right under the foot of Migma Mountain and had consequently been spared the destruction from the blowout. They formed a very old forest, graceful and dark as a cathedral, with almost no understorey. Cool and calm, they were an enormous contrast to the broken swamp, bluffs, boulder fans and raging creeks of the rest of the area.

Now, I wanted to try for Pandemonium Pass again, this time from Success Lakes. I had poured over the topo maps countless times. It seemed as though much of the distance between the lakes and the pass was the gently sloping shelf above the treeline that I had already observed. Around the lakes themselves, some rather wiggly and tight contour lines indicated country that might be a bit more broken, but people hiked through there every couple of years, so it surely couldn't be too bad. Two men had made a tragic trip after their three companions had been killed in an avalanche, but that had been in May. In August there would be no risk of that.

This would be an expedition of several days. A decade earlier I might have tried it alone, but I now felt it would be wise to have company. Paul and Jan were easily persuaded to come to Nuk Tessli again. Both were fit and experienced in the wilds of Canada. Paul had made three canoeing expeditions in the arctic, one of them solo. A friend of theirs, also an experienced hiker, apparently, was to come along as well. The plan was for them to fly to Nuk Tessli in a Beaver to pick up me and the dogs, and then we would all continue to Success Lakes. The extra flying time was only about ten minutes. They would bring their food; I would bring rations for me and my animals. I would provide the maps, and they would bring a satellite phone.

I like to fly as early as possible so I don't have to think about it for too long, but my friends were late and I was wound up tight when they finally arrived. Still, the day was cool and not too windy and the flight was calm. Because of my dislike of flying, I have never done the fabled flightseeing tour; our route went over part of it. After a few minutes, the land fell away into the trench, like the bottom falling out of the world. I could not help but think of the countless hours of bush bashing I had done to cover that distance on foot. The long ribbon of Knot Lake lay below, slightly bluey green and opaque. We entered the little valley of Success Creek. We were flying quite high, and all of a sudden were faced with a huge wall of ice dimly seen through storm clouds. On our left, seemingly no more than a wingtip away, was a small gem-green lake nestled in a wall of moraine. The other side of the valley seemed steep and rocky, but there was no time to look properly. Far below was another lake, barely distinguishable from the grey rocks that surrounded it, looking incredibly tiny. This was our destination. It was quite a lot lower than Nuk Tessli, being only one thousand metres in altitude. With rain splattering on the plane windows, we spiralled down and landed.

I had heard a lot of stories about this lake. For many years an American had flown in there for the summer. He was seemingly quite an eccentric. Locals with their own planes who visited him told me that he had plywood cutouts of bar girls in front of his camp. Other friends, who flew in there to make an attempt on Monarch Mountain, were told by the eccentric that they were not allowed to camp on "his" lake. He had no legal right to say that to them, but there were no tent sites except around his shack and so the climbers moved on. A geologist acquaintance, though, said that although the American was a bit odd, he was quite friendly. The geologist was shown what appeared to be human bones; there were all sorts of rumours floating around that the American had killed someone. I've never taken much notice of rumours. Some years after I started Nuk Tessli, a friend told me she had overheard a bunch of local guys discussing my attempt to start a resort in the high country. Because I was a lone female, they came to the conclusion I was going to operate orgies up there.

It had been some years since the American had occupied his shack. A couple of crude logs jutting into the water had done duty as his dock. We had to leap onto them from the plane's floats; they dipped and rolled but we got the very heavy packs safely onto dry land. There were no plywood bargirls to greet us, but a platform and a couple of rotting tarps lay buried in the trees. Although we had seen such spectacular country before we had landed, the view from the platform was down the creek, and little was visible past the grey lake but the steep sides of the valley and the forested hills beyond the trench. The valley was narrow with limited sunlight—not a place I would want to spend a great deal of time. The pilot fired up his aircraft and took off. It was not a very big lake and had only one approach. The pilot would not be able to lift off the water with more than one passenger aboard. The only way out of here was to walk.

Success Lakes

Our original plan had been to camp at this site for a couple of days and explore from there before moving on. But it was such an uninteresting spot, we shouldered our heavy packs and started to hike. It seemed very likely that the American would have cut a trail farther up the creek; if he hadn't explored the country, what on earth would he have done with himself in there?

We immediately ran into trouble. We floundered for a long time on the swampy shore, trying to find any indication of a trail, but we ended up bush bashing through some horrible stuff. I had two dogs at that point. Bucky had been passed on to my Burnaby friends, and Raffi had been put down because of a twisted gut. Now Badger, a shaggy black Rottweiler-coloured rescue from the SPCA, and Nahanni, a white husky from Inuvik who had not pulled her weight in the sled, were my two companions. Both were fairly new to backpacking. I had been training them on day hikes all summer, but this was the first heavy-duty trip that they had been faced with. They were finding the tangles of bush really difficult. They had to be coaxed and yanked over obstacles, and that delayed us further.

At last we found signs of an old trail. Rotten remnants of cut logs were scattered among weathered chainsaw blazes on trees. The trail was very overgrown, but it was easy enough to follow, and we were finally able to climb out of the swampy undergrowth beside the lake. It was a very curious forest that we were walking through—almost every tree was deformed. The trees themselves were no more than three or four metres high, but each bulged with burls that completely surrounded the trunk and branches like beads strung on a stem. It was a sunless forest, dull and gloomy, and the distortions gave it an eerie feel.

We climbed steadily until we reached a rockslide. The trail vanished. There was not a single sign that anyone had ever walked this way. The rockslide was loose and steep and not at all easy to negotiate. Once again the dogs were having major problems. We tried to drop below the boulders but got tangled in impassable bush again. The dogs would get stuck and hung up and turned over. In the end, Paul took Nahanni's pack on top of his own, and I struggled with Badger's.

We reached thinner forest interspersed with half-overgrown rockslides, but they were very steep. We were definitely climbing, but oh how slowly! It was a lot rougher than I expected. Then: "A glacier! A glacier!" Paul called. We struggled to his viewpoint. Ahead, through a web of branches, we could see a startlingly turquoise lake backed by a dirty scribble of ice tumbling between black rocks half-hidden by a grey mass of cloud. A creek ran from the small glacier and fanned out in a little gravel bar, which appeared to be the only break in the vegetation around the edge of the lake. Through binoculars, I could see pink patches of what I assumed was mountain fireweed beside the creek. It is a common plant along river gravel, and it often grows in great profusion at high altitudes near snow and ice. It sometimes occurs in such large patches that it can be seen from great distances. One August day while hiking over the alpine stretch to the road, I met with the trapper, who was in the area at that time of year working as a guide for the outfitter. He was moving camp in between clients. We might run into each other only once or twice a year so we generally had a good visit. When we did, his horses were happy to crop the short vegetation while we stopped and traded gossip. At one point, the trapper said, "There's them purple flowers." He indicated a mountain behind me. His distance eyesight was much better than mine—I needed binoculars to pick them out. But indeed, "them purple flowers" covered an enormous area. The mountain must have been at least ten kilometres away.

When we came upon the turquoise lake, we had been hiking for several hours. We debated about camping where we were, but nothing was horizontal and we would have had a hard time finding two tent spots. "I want to go to the beach," said someone. I suspected that the little gravel fan wasn't exactly a beach, but loved the idea of being so close to the flowers, so I was happy to agree.

The distance was not great—no more than a kilometre or two, but it took several more hours. The vegetation was now not much more than head height, but it was a nightmare to get through. I have never been a fast walker and was soon trailing far behind everyone else. Both dogs stayed with me and I would sometimes carry one of their packs, and sometimes the other. I finally emerged onto the little boulder fan to see the two women grimly moving boulders around in spitting rain to try to make a place flat enough for their tent. "Paul has twisted his foot," they informed me. He was sitting by the icy creek with his foot in the water, trying to reduce the swelling. It was already twice its normal size. He had apparently grabbed hold of a branch for support and it had broken, causing him to fall. He had dumped his pack and limped to the campsite. When we had the tents up, the three of us went back to find the pack and share his heavy load.

Paul's group cooked on a little fuel stove; I prepared my rations on a small fire, as I have always done on backpacking trips. There were suitable stones right beside the waterfront: I removed some so that after I had finished with the firepit I could cover it with the rocks again and render it invisible. It was a scramble to get a meal

Camp by Upper Success Lake.

before dark. The whole distance we had travelled was no more than four kilometres. It had taken nine hours.

I was up early as always, and the morning was halfway sunny. I could not wait to explore the creek. I plunged into the terrible bush again, but now that I was going away from the lake, it lasted only fifteen minutes, then opened up to half-overgrown moraines. They were quite loose in places but blessedly easy going after the terrible hike of the day before.

There is nothing that gives me more joy than discovering flowers in new alpine settings. Almost at once, I hit a large patch of the fireweed mixed with Indian paintbrush. The red and purple vibrated and were a fabulous foil to the swirling, slightly opaque, greyish water and wet granite boulders. This was nothing to what the creek had in store for me, however. It proved to be quite the most stunning alpine garden I have ever seen. The blooms were in their prime. Brilliant red paintbrush, purple mountain fireweed, yellow arnica, blue lupin, mauve mountain daisies, all jumbled in profusion and glowing with the fresh, slightly hazy morning sun. The light was a photographer's dream. Almost every picture had either the brilliantly turquoise lake or the magnificent tumbling ice as a background. Less showy flowers included masses of the purple-blossomed insectivore called butterwort, and mountain sorrel with its tart, fresh leaves to nibble on.

Butterwort.

Butterwort is a special plant for me. An English flower book I had as a kid described it as being very rare in the British Isles. I was thrilled to stumble upon a struggling specimen while hiking in the north of England in my late teens. I never saw it again or even thought about it for decades—and then I discovered it at Nuk Tessli. Here, and in other damp alpine areas I have come across, it was abundant. There were thousands of them. Their lime-green leaves are covered with soft, slimy bristles. Bugs are attracted by their sweet smell and become bogged in the slime. Slowly, the plant digests them. A number of species of insectivorous plants inhabit these mountains. Granite produces acidic soils, which tie up nitrogen in such a way that the plants have trouble accessing it. Mechanisms for trapping and digesting insects gives the plants an edge in these hostile ecosystems. And there is certainly no lack of insects!

Davidson's penstemon.

Close to the glacier I also found species I had not seen all that often: a dwarf yellow monkeyflower; a wonderful clump of mist maiden, which I had encountered only in Gentian Valley before; and there, on a drier, flatter area, was the Davidson's penstemon. We were still quite a distance from Pandemonium Pass but seeing it here was a confirmation that I had been on the right track.

The glacier cascaded into a little pool and that was as far as I was able to go. I was now quite high above our neon-vivid lake. Far to my left, glimpses of incredibly rugged peaks reared over swirls of fog. On the far side of the lake, more fog hung about the mountains, but I could see where Pandemonium Pass must be. A ridge hid part of the route over there, but the long alpine shelf I had seen from the pass itself was visible and it obviously would not be a problem. As long, that is, as Paul could walk.

I arrived back at camp late morning to find that the others were only recently out of bed and making their first meal. I have always been baffled by people's ability to sleep in, particularly while the sun is shining. Paul's foot was still swollen. I had brought a first aid kit and in it was an aluminum splint, which we strapped over his shoe with duct tape. This meant he could cautiously get about. It would appear that there was nothing broken. We expected to use five days' food to hike to Hunlen Falls from this place, and had ten days' food all together, so we could afford to wait at the lake for a while longer. I had arranged for Tweedsmuir Air to pick me up at Hunlen Falls and fly me back to Nuk Tessli. The others planned to hike down the major tourist trail from the campsite to Highway 20. The trail comes out at the bottom of the Hill. They had taken their vehicle down there before they had flown into the mountains.

But what would we do if Paul couldn't walk? He now confessed that he had not brought the satellite phone. He had checked it before he left, found that his subscription had expired, and didn't bother to renew it. No one would miss us until we failed to turn up near Hunlen Falls in ten days' time. None of us could stomach the hike back to where we had landed, and in any case, we would still have to go the extra distance to Knot Lake to get picked up. Climbing friends who had hiked down that creek told me they were constantly bluffed—it sounded much the same as Pandemonium Creek, so it was not a good choice either. Also, no one would be expecting us to go that way.

Jan proposed that she and I should scout out a route toward Pandemonium Pass. We left the dogs in camp to give ourselves a bit more freedom of movement. We waded the creek (the stones were slippery with glacial slime) then scrambled above the trees to a sloping sea of boulders with pockets of vegetation down among the cracks. Sometimes we stayed on top of the rocks; often we had to drop between them, then climb again. Slow going, but we gradually approached what appeared to be a pass. Concubine Peak and our small glacier reared on our left, while a hummocky hill of rock lay on our right. The half-hearted sunshine continued, and the hike was quite pleasant.

As we reached the pass, however, we were suddenly battered by a bitter cold wind. Hastily pulling on coats, we fought our way into it, and an incredible panorama was revealed. An enormous sheet of ice, many kilometres long, swung down in a big curve from mountains that were hidden in storm clouds. This was the Talchako Glacier, one of many swooping down from the Monarch Icefield. I had seen it on the map, of course, but nothing prepared me for its grandeur. In any case, the maps I had were not always accurate: much of the information was fifty years out of date and I had discovered many discrepancies. Most glaciers had shrunk so much in that time, the end of it could have been anywhere, but it seemed to be more or less where the map had indicated. There was no way we were getting down onto it, though. Below us was a cliff followed by at least a one-hundred-metre drop of suicidally steep moraine. We stayed high a little longer, fighting the wind, but if we wanted to get back to camp before dark we would have to return.

Paul was hobbling around the boulder fan when Jan and I arrived at the creek. Thanks to the sunny afternoon, the water was now much deeper and swifter. We shouted instructions to each other about the crossing, but could hardly make ourselves heard above the crashing roar. However, we both made it over without falling in. Getting wet was not a major concern. I didn't want to drown the camera, though.

The weather that summer had been a mix. For a week or so it would be gorgeous, then we would have a week of rain. It was our luck to hit a rainy patch. Paul's group had brought in a tarp and ropes—no wonder their packs had been heavy, but now they were very welcome, for the next day it rained and blew miserably. The tarp gave us some respite, but the wind blew straight across the boulder fan. It drove rain underneath the tarp, and took with it the heat from our fire.

While waiting in camp, we were entertained by a young dipper. These robin-sized birds have evolved to take advantage of a very specialized niche in nature. Although they look nothing like a water bird, their feathers are so dense, they form a waterproof coat. The dipper inhabits fast mountain streams and feeds on underwater insects. It can tolerate very cold conditions because the dense feather coat traps air. This might seem a handicap for an underwater bird, but it counteracts that by having long toes that grasp the stones on the stream bed. I see them at Nuk Tessli most winters, living among the canyons of frozen spray where broken water boils too fast to freeze. They usually breed in the alpine.

They are called dippers because they evince a jerking, bobbing motion. Perhaps it is something to do with trying to judge depth through swiftly flowing water. Our young entertainer was still being fed by its parents. It was adult-sized, but still had fat yellow baby lips. While waiting for its meals on wheels, it was practising how to dip. Its bobbing seemed to be a reflex that was a tad uncoordinated, as if it was puzzled as to why its limbs would go into these strange spasms.

On day three the rain abated again. Paul's foot was improving but unless we found a very easy route, he would not be able to hike out. I dimly remembered that a ground-to-air emergency signal was a cross. We weighed everything red that we could find with boulders—rain pants, plastic bags and so on—and arranged them into our signal. Fortunately, Paul's tent was also a brilliant red. If we heard a plane, we would all wave bright things frantically. I learned early on in my hiking career that you never wave to an aircraft except in an emergency. I have heard instances of enthusiastic hikers thinking they were having fun waving, then finding themselves with a bill for the rescue chopper. With a bit of luck, if anyone saw us, they would take us seriously.

Taking advantage of the clearer weather, Jan and I set off to see if we could find another route out. A rockslide to the right of where we had gone before looked as though it would give us a passage through the bush. To our surprise, after we crossed the creek (which was back down to its cool morning level) we picked up a bit of a trail along the shore. It took us to the rockslide we were aiming for. The boulders on the slide were bathtub-sized with deep cracks in between them. We weren't sure how the dogs would manage them (we had left them at camp again), but it was not too bad for us to scramble up. If we found easy going after the slide, it would be worth coaxing the dogs through. Not far along, a huge overhanging boulder reared up against one side of the slide. The little trail, almost vertical at this point, seemed to lead to it.

To our immense surprise, we found what appeared to have been someone's home. Until now, it had seemed as though we were the only humans ever to fight our way through this wild and impenetrable country. Under the overhang, rocks had been piled to make a rough wall at the windward end, and a small plywood platform had been installed. A long iron pipe as wide as a torso had been laid on a bed of stones nearby. A chimney had been welded at one end and a metal flap at the other—obviously an attempt at a stove. Hanging on a tree was a tiny, plastic-framed shaving mirror with half the silvering missing off the back. On another was hooked an old-model geologist's hammer. The most bizarre item sat in the middle of the plywood platform. It was a rocking chair.

It was obvious that someone had spent a lot of time here, although not very recently. It was impossible to land a plane on this upper lake, so whoever had created this shelter must have had his supplies flown to the boulder fan by helicopter. He would then have carried everything along the shore to his shelter. Presumably, he had found the bivvy rock during earlier explorations; it had not been visible until we were standing right under it. I doubt the shelter had been created by our friend of the lower lake, for the whole tone of this place was different. It was tidy, and very well organized. It was likely engineered by a prospector. We were in country that was probably beyond the boundary of the Tweedsmuir Provincial Park, and some of the rocks around had very different shapes and colours from the usual pale granite of the Coast Range.

The land opened up and now we found a fairly easy route up a dry gully. This looked promising. We were climbing the rocky hill that had been to our right on our previous hike. Soon we could see the glacier again. It was hot, rather muggy, and windless. Today the mountains were more or less clear. The rugged peaks looked less dramatic when they were not playing hide and seek among the clouds. From the top of the little hill, we had a really good view of the ground in between us and Pandemonium Pass. The long shelf lay enticingly along the side of the mountain, but before it was a nightmare of cliffs and enormous moraines. The map had shown a few irregular contours around both Success Lakes, but there had been nothing to indicate such broken country. With some difficulty we found our way down the hill. Sometimes goats make trails on top of moraines and they are reasonably easy to walk on. Jan scrambled up, but the top was knife-edged and extremely loose. It seemed that even goats had found this place too inhospitable.

We wandered around a bit but could find no way through suitable for four middle-aged-plus hikers, one very lame, and two dogs. I wondered how climbers who had done this route had managed, but I guess they'd had the experience and the equipment to cope.

Back at camp, the others were beginning to get a little antsy at our lack of progress. Paul admitted that the satellite phone snafu was his fault, but he accused me of not researching the route properly. It was no good blaming the maps. We should have asked our pilot to give us a little tour around, but the weather had not been good and in any case, it is very difficult to see details from the air.

I was more used to the rhythms of the bush and happier about sitting it out for a few more days. We still had plenty of food. We were camped directly below the route that the flight-seeing tours always took. I was surprised that none had come by so far, but on the first day, fog had clung to the land masses, and on the second and the fourth, rain had socked us in. Day five looked halfway decent again.

I wanted to explore the country south of our camp. According to the map, the main Concubine glacier would swoop down over the next ridge. Once again, the moraine was loose and a little tricky, and the flowers were not so interesting here, but I gained altitude and the turquoise lake was soon spread below. Once more the tantalizing shelf and the peaks around Pandemonium Pass came into view. The vivid red dot of Paul's tent stood out like a glowing coal on the boulder fan.

I was near the top of the ridge when suddenly I heard a small plane. It was coming from Talchako Glacier and veering toward our little lake. It was alarmingly high. Would the pilot notice us? I could see my three companions leaping up and down waving coats. The pilot started to turn in a circle. He waggled his wings to indicate that he had spotted us, then swooped down through the gap above Success Creek.

The others were yelling at me. Their voices were distant, but they carried up the ridge. How could they think that I had not heard or seen the plane? But I wanted to know what was over the ridge. Only a few metres higher. When I reached top, however, there was another ridge, and then another. I could see a bit of the upper part of the glacier I was aiming for, but it was obviously going to be too far for me to reach.

The nearest helicopter was based at Hagensborg, near Bella Coola. This was the one that had flown me into Nuk Tessli. The plane would have taken half an hour to reach Nimpo and if a helicopter was available right away, it could conceivably arrive within a couple of hours. We waited. And we waited. The day stayed rain free, but the clouds began to close in again.

We packed everything except the red tent. Our gear and the dogs were stashed at the edge of the boulder fan, the bored dogs tied to trees. I couldn't risk them running off if the chopper landed. We planned to grab the tent the minute we heard the helicopter. We waited and we waited. It must have been six hours before it came. It was not the six-seater AStar from Hagensborg, but a four-seater RCMP helicopter that had been deployed all the way from Kamloops. The AStar would have come across Talchako Glacier, but this machine flew up the creek.

Because of the dogs, there was not enough room for all of us inside. The pilot said that maybe one or two of us could walk down Success Creek. He ventured that it hadn't looked too bad from the air. The others looked mutinous and I certainly didn't want to attempt it on my own. So in the end, the dogs and I were flown back to Nuk Tessli first. Although I dislike being in a fixed-wing plane, for some reason I quite enjoy helicopters. So it was a treat to rattle down Success Creek, cross the Trench, swoop over Boundary Lake, and touch down in the little meadow near the cabins. Not long after I had arrived at Nuk Tessli, I had cleared a few small trees to make an area for a helicopter to land in case of emergencies. It seemed quite large on the ground but it looked pretty tiny from the air. However, the pilot had no difficulty in landing. He didn't turn off the motor; I ducked and ran across the meadow clutching the dogs' leads (the tail rotor is dangerous because it is invisible) and away went the chopper to pick up my friends. He took them straight to the bottom of the Hill, where they could recover their vehicle. I was expecting a bill from the government for the helicopter ride, but none was forthcoming. Apparently, rescues are free.

Knot Lake Fire

From: Chris Czajkowski
To: <dave.smith@gov.bc.ca> *
Sent: August 1, 2009, 3:14 PM
Subject: Fire near Elbow Lake

*I have a resort halfway between Charlotte Lake and
the southern tip of Tweedsmuir Park. I am alarmed to
see smoke pouring up from the big trench somewhere
between Knot Lake and Lonesome Lake. Probably right
around Elbow Lake. A big lightning storm passed over
there yesterday evening.*

*This is 7–10 kms west of my resort; a stiff south-
west wind is blowing. I have four guests. The only way
we can get out of here is to fly via charter from Nimpo
Lake. I have no phone, only a radiophone that can be
reached from a local channel at Nimpo Lake—if anyone
is listening. I will switch the phone on; you can contact
me via the Nimpo Lake Resort or the Anahim Airport (I
have the same frequency).*

*So far everything is OK here but this fire could be
potentially dangerous to me and my property, given the*

---

*   Name has been changed.

*violent southwest winds that can happen here. I lived
through the Lonesome Lake Fire of 2004.*
   Chris

....

When I first came to Nuk Tessli, the summers were pleasant, often hot but usually tempered by a cool breeze; the high temperature rarely lasted through the night. Once or twice a year, we would have a heat wave, but these never lasted more than a day or two. In the winter, there would be one to two metres of snow around the cabins. Early in the summer, June and July, Nuk Tessli would bear the brunt of stupendous thunderstorms with lightning crashing into the hills, trees struck and hail or heavy rain so loud on the roof I could hardly hear myself think. I found these storms quite terrifying, but they were always accompanied by heavy rain and there was no risk of fire.

During my first August, when I was still living in a tent, the country filled with smoke. It was a very still day. The sun was burnished to bronze and I couldn't see across the lake. I had no radiophone at that time, no Internet, nor any other means of communication. Would people even know I was here and might need rescuing? I prepared a five-gallon bucket of food, a box with journals and irreplaceable books, and the chainsaw and a few other tools. I had constructed a crude log wharf by that point, and I tied the canoe to it, with the bucket of supplies beside it, prepared to bail out if necessary. The lake had a few small islands in it, and the forest on these was much older; presumably they had survived the more recent fires in the area. The islands, I figured, would be my best bet in an emergency.

Within twenty-four hours, however, the smoke vanished. The next time I went out for mail, I learned that the sawmill at Anahim Lake had burned down. The smoke had travelled at least sixty kilometres and had not been a problem anywhere else; it was a fluke of the wind that had carried it to Nuk Tessli.

As the years progressed, the spring thunderstorms abated. Winter snow levels dropped, a metre now being as much as we would get. Summers got hotter and drier. Heat waves now lasted for weeks. The year 2003 was a terrible year for fires in BC. Parts of Kelowna and Barrier were destroyed, and there were a couple of major blazes in the Chilcotin. But the prevailing wind came to Nuk Tessli from the coast and the smoke hardly touched my lake. A slight haze gave the mountains a bluish cast, but that was it. The flower meadows fried quickly, though. I was expecting a reporter and photographer from *Beautiful British Columbia* magazine on July 31. On July 29 I hiked to the Mammaries and found the meadows calendar-picture perfect. I was delighted to think that my gorgeous flowers might be portrayed in a magazine that went around the world. But when I took the photographer up there three days later, the flowers had shrivelled and browned.

The following year, the snow level was low and the weeks-long heat wave started early. On June 21, a lightning strike initiated a fire not far from Hunlen Falls in the Tweedsmuir Provincial Park. It was a good forty kilometres away, on the far side of the trench, so I was not initially worried about it, but Nuk Tessli was downwind and we received a lot of smoke. Once more, many BC communities were in trouble—Kelowna was threatened again—and neither Parks, nor Forestry, nor Fish and Wildlife figured our local fire was important. A month later, however, it had fizzed and spluttered its way over the ridge between it and the trench, and it started to travel down the steep slope to Lonesome Lake. Up on top, it would have been easy to control. Once it reached the precipitous valley walls, it was too dangerous to stop. Steep mountain walls act like chimneys. Thermals rise against them— which is why eagles and condors often spiral close to them. Fire exacerbates these hot, rising winds and makes it too dangerous for aircraft to get anywhere near.

July 21 was graced with a hot, strong southwest wind, and the fire took off. The east branch of the Atnarko River valley lay right along the wind's path. The fire roared up it and consumed eighteen kilometres of steep, wild river valley in two days. It burned all the buildings near Lonesome Lake: the original Edwards homestead, Jack and Trudy's barns and house and the cabin that I had built across the river from them. Fortunately, the Turners no longer lived there; they had moved down into the Bella Coola Valley not long after I had left. Trudy's brother, John, however, still called Ralph's old claim home. The house and the family history that was stored there were destroyed.

The fire was big news nationally. That was the year I installed satellite Internet and I was inundated by people wishing me well, newspaper reporters wanting news and client cancellations. The whole area was thick with smoke and it was hard for anyone to find out what was going on. Planes couldn't fly, and at times it was even too dangerous for helicopters. On July 25, clients who had arrived the day Lonesome Lake was burned flew back to Nimpo. Smoke had prevented them from leaving on time, but then a breeze started from the west and cleared the air enough to allow them to take off. Only two wwoofers and I remained at Nuk Tessli. The whole of the rest of the country for sixty kilometres all around had been evacuated.

The lovely little breeze that had finally revealed the mountains to us was a double-edged sword, however. Unbeknown to us at first, it was stirring up the fire between Nuk Tessli and Nimpo. I was enjoying the view up the lake and the unaccustomed pleasure of having a blue sky, and it was only when I went to the outhouse and looked to the north that I saw a huge pall of smoke lit orange by flames. It seemed to be just over the next ridge. I radiophoned Nimpo (the locals were keeping the channel open) and they said they didn't know what was happening. They could see nothing but smoke. All they knew was that it was big. I asked my contact to get Tweedsmuir Air to send a plane in as soon as possible.

After the lightning strike a month previously, I had packed a box of irreplaceables and added a couple of pieces of paper. One listed the most important things I would have to take out, cameras, computers, etc., and the other noted items that would be expensive to replace, such as the chainsaw. The box had become largely unpacked as I kept using items out of it, but the lists meant that everything could be reassembled quickly. The plane came within half an hour, and there was no room for anything but essentials. The smoke had bronzed the sky and tendrils were already filling the air above the lake. The pilot flew us right into the smoke and above the fire, which was active on several fronts. The flames were taller than the trees they were burning. The fire was completely out of control.

By then a camp for hundreds of firefighters and several helicopters had mushroomed at the Anahim Lake airport. All who could do so stayed at resorts. I was lucky that I had a place of my own, even if it was only the hated Nimpo cabin. While thus incarcerated, I wrote passionately about the terrors of the experience, and that became the framework for *Wildfire in the Wilderness*.

The thing about fire is the not knowing what is going to happen. Smoke makes it very difficult to see what is going on. My valley was spared the flames and, nine days later when the weather cooled a little, I was allowed home. Nuk Tessli and its valley were to be plagued by smoke for another month, but the fire was no longer a danger to me.

. . . .

And now, in 2009, I was going through exactly the same thing again. Even the dates were identical. Oddly enough, since the hot summers had been more consistent, we never had the violent spring thunderstorms that had occurred during my early years at Nuk Tessli. Instead, we would get fairly moderate rumbles that were not usually very frightening later in the summer. And yet these were far more dangerous than the violent ones, because they came without rain.

Thunderstorms at Nuk Tessli are a war of the winds. If a summer day starts with an east wind, no matter how clear and sunny it is, a thunderstorm is pretty much guaranteed. Often, however, the mountains would be clear and a fresh breeze would blow from the southwest while in the east and north, dark clouds would start to build. If the clouds came close enough, the mountain breeze would suddenly die out; black, silver-edged piles of vapour would start to tumble together from all directions, and the ground wind would instantly change. Sometimes, Nuk Tessli was right between the weather systems. The black clouds would creep closer and closer but they would evaporate before they reached my lake. The storm that arrived on July 31 that year, however, passed directly overhead. It was comparatively gentle, starting with a few distant murmurs and slowly getting closer. It banged once or twice directly overhead, and then calmly receded as it travelled west toward Bella Coola. It was cloudy, with very little wind, and not a drop of rain fell.

The morning of August 1 was clear and sunny. The breeze was freshening again from the west. Eleven people, both clients and wwoofers, flew out in the morning, and four other visitors arrived shortly afterwards. These were a long-time friend, Joyce Dorey, eighty years old, and her son, daughter-in-law and eleven-year-old great-granddaughter. Joyce had visited Nuk Tessli a couple of times before. I left them enjoying the sun on the deck of their cabin while I went to the computer to catch up on office work. It is always a struggle to keep up with business matters when I have a lot of visitors to feed and entertain, and I needed a few hours to tidy up my books. The day was less oppressive than the previous one had been, and the fresh breeze continued to keep the air clear. It seemed unlikely that we would have any more storms.

The computer was situated to allow me a view up the lake. Although the smoke was not too bad at Nuk Tessli, a big fire had been burning for a couple of weeks not far from the lightning strike of 2004. It was on the far side of Turner Lake (which empties into the trench via Hunlen Falls) so I didn't expect it to be a bother to me. The wind was coming from the northwest, and a thick veil of smoke from this fire was blowing in front of the mountains. It seemed, however, that in one particular spot, the smoke was more concentrated. It was quite a while before I could be sure. It looked very much as though there was a fire in the trench. With a growing feeling of dread, I realized that Nuk Tessli could be in serious trouble. The Lonesome Lake fire had been incredibly dramatic, but the worst of it had been two valleys north of Nuk Tessli. This fire might be a great deal smaller, but it was much closer—and it was directly upwind.

From: Dave Smith
To: Chris Czajkowski
Cc: Trevor Johnson*
Sent: August 1, 2009, 3:34 PM
Subject: RE: Fire near Elbow Lake

Please give the location of your cabin either by lat and long or which lake they are at. The area you are talking about is very large so we do not want to make a mistake by making an assumption.

    Please reply so Trevor gets the e-mail as he will be the one responding to you.

    Thanks
    Dave Smith RFT
    Manager
    Cariboo Fire Centre

From: Chris Czajkowski
To: Dave Smith
Cc: Trevor Johnson

---

*   Name has been changed.

Sent: August 1, 2009, 4:15 PM
Subject: RE: Fire near Elbow Lake

Thanks for your quick response.
 I think the fire is approximately 52 degrees 05 north and 125 degrees 40 west.
 This is Elbow Lake. It is in the trench between Knot Lake and Lonesome Lake, right at the south end of the Tweedsmuir Provincial Park.
 Chris

From: Trevor Johnson
To: Chris Czajkowski
Sent: August 1, 2009, 4:38 PM
Subject: RE: Fire near Elbow Lake

I have a patrol plane about 15 minutes away and we are just contacting him to look in the Elbow Lake, Lonesome/Knot Lake area. We have a fire close to the Kidney Lake/Widgeon Lake area. Could this be the one??? I will let you know what we find shortly.

From: Chris Czajkowski
To: Trevor Johnson
Sent: August 1, 2009, 4:40 PM
Subject: RE: Fire near Elbow Lake

The wind is SW on my lake (52 degrees 03 north and 125 degrees 33 west) but the smoke is travelling south. It is completely blocking my view of Migma Mountain although I can still see Mount Monarch through the haze. That is why I do not think it is the Kidney/Widgeon Lake fire (which would be too far north and west).
 Chris

From: Chris Czajkowski
To: Trevor Johnson
Sent: August 1, 2009, 4:53 PM
Subject: RE: Fire near Elbow Lake

*I think I can now see flame-coloured smoke. (It might
be the angle of the sun.) Can you please tell me what is
going on?*

> *Either email or phone the Nimpo Lake Resort. They
can get me on the local radio frequency.*

> *Duncan Stewart at Tweedsmuir Air will know the
exact geography. He cannot get me directly on the radiophone but he can phone the Nimpo Resort and they can
pass on the message.*

> *Chris*

From: Trevor Johnson
To: Chris Czajkowski
Sent: August 1, 2009, 5:02 PM
Subject: RE: Fire near Elbow Lake

*Hello, our patrol plane has picked up the fire you are
referring to I believe. We have a heli heading to the site
to give us a better assessment and check on values in the
immediate area. Please note this fire is in the Coastal
fire centre's response area but the Cariboo Fire Centre is
doing the assessment. Our heli will be coming to land at
your location.*

At this point I told my visitors what was going on. The deck in
front of their cabin did not have a view of the big mountains,
and they had been enjoying what seemed to them a peaceful,
sunny afternoon beside the sparkling waters of the lake. I didn't
want to alarm them, but it was hard for me to put on a calm,

Knot Lake fire. Boundary Lake below.

unworried face. Inside, my stomach was churning. I knew very
well how unpredictable fires could be. Once the Lonesome Lake
fire reached the upper Atnarko River, it had galloped eighteen
kilometres in two days. If my estimate was correct, this fire was
only half that distance away. If the wind swung to the southwest,
we would be directly in its path.

It was quite a while before the promised helicopter landed
in the little meadow behind the cabin. The motor was switched
off and three people disembarked. "The fire is on the far side of
Knot Lake," I was informed, a little bit more south than I had
estimated. "At the moment," the fire official continued, "you
have Knot Lake in between, but it's very close to the head of the
lake and could easily cross the valley. You will have to leave."

Even though I had expected it, I could not believe this was
happening again. This time there had been no early warning so I

had not prepared any lists. I simply threw everything together and hoped for the best. The clients had not even properly unpacked, so they were soon ready. They had brought in all kinds of produce. It seemed silly to use up precious plane space to fly it out, but if I left it, it would rot and attract bears.

"Your guys were just in here," I emailed Trevor Johnson. "They said the fire is actually at the head of Knot Lake. They told me that the smoke was expected to get pretty bad and the fire would likely be here in two to four days, so we are flying out as soon as possible. Duncan is going to try and get a plane to us in about an hour and a half.

"I am taking my computer apart and will be in touch as soon as I get my email set up again, probably tomorrow."

Once again, Tweedsmuir Air arrived promptly. Once again, it was already early evening. The sun was low behind the column of smoke, backlighting it dramatically and painting the plane's wing burnished orange. As we began to power up the lake, I snatched a last look at the cabins. Would I ever see them again? We lifted off and our greater height revealed more of the smoke column, but we turned before it was possible to see into the trench.

We landed at Nimpo uneventfully, but they were not smoke free as a big fire had erupted at the top of the Hill. Three others burned in the Bella Coola Valley, all triggered by the same lightning storm.

Fire Watch at Ginty Creek

Highway 20 was blocked by two fires farther east as well as the one on the top of the Hill, so Nimpo Lake and Anahim Lake were cut off. The fire near Alexis Creek, an hour west of Williams Lake, was so bad everyone was evacuated. It was a struggle to find accommodation for my friends as everywhere was full of stranded people and firefighters. Although the air was thick with smoke, I could still drive to my new property at Ginty Creek. It was dark by this time and a full moon hung in the sky. The smoke had turned it blood red.

It was once more a time of great anxiety. For several days, visibility was severely compromised, and my throat was raw with smoke. Most of that came from a couple of fires to the north of my place. They were not all that far away, but the winds from that direction are rarely strong, which is why the smoke was not moving. The advantage was that it would be unlikely to fan the fire. The wind then swung to the dreaded southwest and began to pick up speed. That worried me further, but it did clear the smoke away, and when I contacted various fire officials they were surprised to hear about it because it was quite calm elsewhere.

BC Forest Service maintained a couple of informational web-sites regarding the fires, but when they got really busy, these sites were not always updated. In any case, only the larger fires were recorded. I managed to find a US Forest Service heat sensor web-site for the whole of North America. The signals were bounced from satellites and the site was reconfigured every few hours. It recorded every fire since the beginning of the year. Yellow splotches indicated burns that were either out or under control, orange showed increased activity and red showed violence. Most of central BC was suffering, particularly areas around Clinton on Highway 97, which was surrounded by three very large and active fires. The main north/south route through the province was therefore periodically closed as well as Highway 20.

My little fire was a pinprick on the map, but it was glowing red. Normally, it would be so remote and insignificant that the forest service would have ignored it. If it hadn't been for its place-ment directly upwind of Nuk Tessli, it would have been allowed to wander at will.

With the US Forest Service's satellite information, I was able to pinpoint the fire exactly. It was where I had camped at the head of Knot Lake when I had tried to go up the creek to Pandemonium Pass. It was burning the mature stand of cedar, one of the only pieces of forest in the bottom of the valley that had been spared the blowout of Pandemonium Creek. That won-derful, cathedral-like gloom was now being reduced to ashes.

The day after I flew out, there was a meeting at the Nimpo Lake Hall for people concerned about the fires. A man named Larry had been brought into the area as a fire coordinator but he was from Saskatchewan and knew nothing of the local geog-raphy. The firefighting services use computer models to predict weather and their forecasts were for rain. But us locals looked at the sky and shook our heads. At one point Larry talked about a "six-inch rain" that had fallen at the top of the Hill. "There were six inches between each drop," he said.

He told me that sprinklers were going to be installed at Nuk Tessli the following day. He asked me if the cabins were enclosed at the bottom. The buildings had no proper foundations: they were simply erected on rocks. I had left space under the sill logs so that the wind would get under there and keep the foundations dry. This was a potentially dangerous situation because sparks could get into the dry litter beneath. The sprinkler crew would have to give the crawlspace a good soaking.

That evening I received the following email:

From: Trevor Johnson
To: Chris Czajkowski
Sent: August 2, 2009, 8:26 PM
Subject: Permission to set up sprinkler protection units

Hello Chris, please read the below statement and let me know what your thoughts are.

Please note that the Wildlife Management Branch, Cariboo Fire Center anticipates wildfire activity on or near your privately held property. The Wildfire Management Branch is willing to implement initial fire mitigation activities on your property in anticipation of fire reaching your property. Please understand that wildfire is anticipated to reach your property, however this not a certainty due to the nature of the wildfire and weather. The possibility exists that mitigation efforts could be implemented with the intention of protection and the fire not reach the property. Also, the Wildlife Management Branch cannot guarantee any degree of success from mitigation efforts.

With permission, wildfire suppression activities will ensue on your property. Potential activities may include the initial implementation and some maintenance of any or all of the following:

The removal of fuel sources resulting in the possible falling of trees or brush, clearing of wood piles or other fuel around structures, and/or digging of fire guard resulting in possible soil disruption.

The setup of structure protection sprinkler systems and/or hose base watering resulting in possible water damage to the structures and property or soil erosion.

Possible cleanup from mitigation activities may be necessary; however, these activities are not within the capability of the Wildfire Management Branch.

The Wildfire Management Branch thanks you for your cooperation.

Do you give permission for the Wildfire Management Branch crews to implement fire suppression activities on your property considering potential consequences?

Should you have any questions, concerns or comments please feel free to contact me at the number below.

Trevor Johnson RFT
Senior Protection Officer
Cariboo Fire Centre.

From: *Chris Czajkowski*
To: *Trevor Johnson*
Sent: *August 3, 2009, 6:09 AM*
Subject: *RE: Permission to set up sprinkler protection units*

I agree to any of the fire suppression implementations recorded below. I understand that there may be damage to the immediate environment and the buildings, even if the fire does not reach them, and that I will have to deal with that myself.

Thank you,
Chris

The following day, Trevor Johnson told me in an email that the sprinkler crew had been diverted to Turner Lake where a lodge had boats to save, but they were continuing to monitor my fire. With so much major activity everywhere, my little blaze was not always checked, and I begged any pilot, private or commercial, who might be anywhere in the area to give me a report. (Some people flew around the fires for fun.) I continued to look at the US Forest Service heat sensor site, and, against all odds, the Knot Lake fire, while still glowing vivid red, did not seem to have crossed the trench.

I began to wonder if I should try to fly in and rescue some of my possessions. I had no fire insurance. The premiums would have been out of sight for a place like Nuk Tessli. I possessed many nature reference books it would be expensive to replace, and things like albums of photos, guest books full of visitors' stories, poems and drawings and costly tools like the chainsaw. I might even try to bring out some food. I don't bother to store much at Ginty Creek during the summer as the first thing I usually do at the end of the tourist season is drive to Williams Lake. But the road was closed; the city supermarkets were out of my reach. Local stores had a paltry selection of rubbery, weeks-old produce at the best of times; they soon ran out and now the freight trucks couldn't get through to resupply them. All the packaged food in the local stores was useless to me because I am sensitive to chemicals. At Nuk Tessli a good thousand dollars' worth of edibles, much of it specific to my preferred diet, was stacked in the attic.

I phoned the two float plane companies that were operating that year and asked if they were likely to fly in my direction and could therefore give me a cheaper ride. Each flight would normally cost $450, but if I could share the plane with someone it would help. Duncan said he could take me in on the evening of the following day and pick me up the next morning. I would get a deal on the first flight, but not on the return trip. Sid said he would charge me full price but fly me in really early and wait for me for two or three hours. This was a great offer as I knew he would also help carry everything down to the wharf.

But miraculously, the temperature dropped and it was now ten degrees cooler. Everything was still hazy with smoke, but it must have been cloudy overhead because it even drizzled a little. The sprinkler crew, I was informed, had now set up their equipment around Nuk Tessli.

And through it all, although it continued to glow red every afternoon on the heat sensor map, the fire stayed on the west side of the trench. I visualized these great old cedars, roaring like torches. Why was a fire of such intensity not crossing the trench? I began to realize that it must be Pandemonium Creek that was holding it back. That wild stream, which had defeated my efforts to climb to the pass, was now my salvation. From the air, the creek would have looked insignificant, and the observers, fighting poor visibility due to smoke, would have dismissed it. Even I could not believe such a narrow piece of water could block such an intense fire.

On August 9, I was told that it had showered heavily at Nuk Tessli and on the surrounding mountains. I would be able to fly in as soon as I liked. Highway 20 was now open in the east, and two wwoofers had made it to Ginty Creek. They would come home with me. I wondered what kind of firefighting damage I would have to deal with: trees cut or building interiors soaked? The two young women would be a great help getting it cleared up.

I wanted to go in on the morning of the tenth as afternoons are generally much bumpier. But a client, a man with three children who should have arrived on the sixth, was running out of vacation time and was determined to go on the afternoon of the ninth. So the wwoofers and I presented ourselves at Sid's float plane base in a blustery, rain-spitting south wind late in the afternoon, and we bumped and shuddered our way to the lake. Visibility was not 100 percent, but now it was due more to the film of rain than to the smoke. A thick haze still curtained the mountains.

We were greeted by the client with his excited kids—they had arrived about half an hour earlier—and five grubby men with hard hats who were waiting for their helicopter. It arrived within a few minutes, a machine that could have transported a dozen people.

From what I could see, there appeared to be very little mess at Nuk Tessli. A few trees had been cut but they were minor. The big difference was the great spider's web of hoses that now snaked all over the property, some large, some small. Twenty-four sprinklers had been set up on high rocks. One by the woodshed had given the firewood a good dampening down. A heavy-duty gas-operated water pump had been installed on the wharf, and another placed on the far side of the point, right where I had pitched my camp while I was building Cabin One. The crew expected to be back every other day or so to run the equipment to make sure everything was working, but the client had been shown how to start the pumps in case of emergencies.

Inside the cabins there was none of the water damage I had dreaded. There was a bit of a mess due to our hasty departure, and some overlooked produce had rotted, but that was all. I set up the computer again. The Internet worked, and we were back in business. Other clients who had been thwarted by the fire were advised of the situation, and in the end I lost only one party.

Right at the end of August, when the fire season could usually be expected to tail off, it grew very hot and dry again. The fire finally jumped Pandemonium Creek. Fortunately, the wind raged from the south, not the southwest, and drove the fire up the trench. I could see the smoke column gradually travelling north. The heat sensor site showed me that it was staying on the west side of the valley—my side was protected by that terrible, beautiful swamp. As long as the wind did not swing, Nuk Tessli would be safe. Eventually the blaze reached the old scar where the Lonesome Lake fire had halted five years before, and burned itself out.

I had lived and hiked in various parts of the trench several times during my explorations of the country. Fire had gone through most of the areas I was familiar with. It would all look very different now.

The Stone Circle

If you hike to the knoll at the top of Long Meadow, where you first see the Mammaries, you are confronted with a flattish plateau that lies in front of the North Ridge. If you head to the tallest point, which is quite a long way to the right of the Mammaries, you will cross the stone circle. It is thirty-four paces from one side to the other and perfectly visible on Google Earth. But it doesn't protrude above the ice-flattened ground any more than the millions of other visible rocks, and a hiker crossing the plateau would be lucky to spot the circle unless he or she knew exactly where it was.

It is, however, quite noticeable from many of the peaks of the North Ridge. It was first pointed out by a friend from North Vancouver, Alan Bell. (It was the Bell family who had "lent" me the come-along.) Alan and I had climbed to the highest point on the ridge, leaving his wife, Elizabeth, and five-year-old Andrew lower down. It was a spitty-rain day and the ice-patched panorama of the Coast Mountains that sprawled across the horizon was dulled by cloud. The plateau stretched below us; its southern edge tipped into the forest that ran down to Nuk Tessli. The circle was whiter than the plateau, and it lay just before where the land fell away.

We didn't examine the circle on that hike—we were more concerned with getting off the mountain in the deteriorating

The mysterious stone circle on the plateau below the Mammaries.

weather—but later I sought it out alone. I remember feeling a distinct reluctance to stand inside it, as if some alien presence still lingered there. Not only was the circle almost completely round, but the rocks that it was composed of were different from those that lay both inside and outside. Their paler colour was not the only factor that distinguished them. Many light-coloured rocks are scattered all over the plateau, but all the ones I have examined are composed of the usual coarse-grained granite. If they were pale, it was because they had not grown a coat of black lichen. Either they had been moved recently by frost or bear action, or they were in an area where the snow lay too late for the lichens to establish themselves. But the circle rocks were composed of different material. They were much finer grained and sharper edged. One side of the ring displayed a few large rocks as big as armchairs, with spaces in between. The majority of the stones, however, were head-sized or smaller, usually flattish, and they formed a dense mass up to two metres across.

The British Columbia geological survey was the first official exploration to go through the area. I met up with the geologists when I was out on a mail trip—they happened to be staying at

Nimpo as well. They had missed the circle entirely, but I was able to show them where it was on their aerial photographs. Once it was pointed out, it was very obvious. Later, I met one of the geologists in Vancouver and showed him samples of the rocks from both inside and outside, and of the circle itself. He opined that the finer grain indicated that the circle rock had been heat-treated after it had originally been formed. He also ventured that the shape was so regular it could not be a natural formation. It must have been man-made.

Alan knew of a museum curator in Vancouver who was interested in man-made circles. We sent him photographs. He was pretty sure it was not man-made. It had to be natural. I was inclined to that opinion for despite its roundness, the stones that composed the circle had no real pattern.

The next time I stood there I pondered all these things. There was plenty of evidence of First Nations occupation at lower elevations, but food passes erratically over the high country and there would have been no reason for people to come up here. Besides, the plateau would have been covered in ice comparatively recently.

With my limited knowledge about such things, I came to the conclusion that it must have been caused by a meteor strike. That would explain the heated rocks. The strike would have occurred before the last ice age and the glacier would have swiped off any superstructure and filled in the middle. Subsequent weathering would leave the rocks exposed. When I put this to the BC geologist, he offered no comment except to say that if pieces of meteorite were lying around they would be worth a great deal of money. They would be obviously different, and very heavy. I examined the area minutely, crawling on hands and knees, but found nothing out of the ordinary apart from the circle itself.

My brother has always been a passionate geologist. I sent him more photographs, using a pink Fanny's Fabrics yardstick to show the size. I also mailed him rock samples. Naturally, I had to backpack these down the mountain and spend money to post them, so they were about as big as apples. "They're no good," my brother wrote. "They need to be head-sized!" I suggested he come and collect his samples himself.

It so turned out that Alan's wife, Elizabeth, was cousin to a man who is now professor emeritus at UBC, and was a geoscientist for the Geological Survey of Canada. Although well into his retirement, cousin Andrew was still a very active hiker. So we arranged an expedition to see the stone circle during the second week of August in 2009. Andrew lived in Canada, but Michael was flying from England so had booked his plane months in advance to get a discount. Then came the fire. Daily, Michael would write and ask, "What is happening? When will you be able to go home?" Daily, I replied, "I haven't a clue!" The weather cooperated in the nick of time and the stone circle expedition could go ahead as planned. I was just as relieved as Michael. Having lived with this mystery for over twenty years, I was very much looking forward to a solution.

We had beautiful weather that August day hiking up to the stone circle. The bit of rain after the fire had cleared the air and there was only a thin haze of smoke. There were five of us: myself, Alan, Elizabeth, Michael and Andrew. We had contacted the museum curator who was interested in man-made circles and although he was keen at first, the fire put him off and he had made other arrangements for his vacation.

All the way up the mountain Michael and Andrew speculated. The word *solifluction* was bandied about. I had never heard it before; it had a comic opera feel, a distinctly flatulent sound. It is apparently a well-known geological term, and when we reached the lookout at the edge of the plateau, the geologists pointed out many examples of it. Solifluction happens when the ground thaws in spring. The surface becomes sloppy and often flows down a slope. It might travel only a few centimetres a year, but eventually obvious loop-shaped or contour-hugging ridges occur. Often several are piled one on top of the other all the way down

Andrew (left) and Michael standing on the Stone Circle.

the slope, like somewhat ragged scales on a fish. I had observed these patterns without understanding them; now that they had been pointed out, I could see them everywhere. Most were covered in tundra, but a few were edged by rocks. But although all of them were curved at the bottom, none formed circles.

"You know, Christine," said my brother in his Prince Charles accent (which he acquired: we didn't grow up speaking like that). "You know, the rocks of the circle are completely different than those on the inside or the outside!" I'd been telling everyone that for years. But, like botanists, geologists take no notice unless you have the right letters after your name.

Michael pooh-poohed my meteor theory. "There are many reasons why this cannot be a meteor strike" he explained. "One is you get a trailing ejecta blanket that surrounds a crater, the edges of which thin away from it. Another is that there would be a hole in the ground. There are many other reasons if you want to get technical about it. None of these are happening here." That made sense, but solifluction didn't quite seem to fit the bill either. Both geologists felt that the next thing to do would be to dig. There would likely be more solid rock underneath and what we were looking at was just the weathered surface.

Along with the pink Fanny's Fabrics yardstick, I had back-packed up my old tree-planting shovel. It is a sturdy tool with a strong shaft and a small blade, ideal for levering up stones. More pictures were taken with the pink yardstick, this time lying beside the geologists who were on their knees grubbing among the rocks. But the foreign stones lay only on the surface. There was nothing beneath them except normal glacial deposits. This made the situation even more puzzling.

A full account of the geologists' paper was published in the *Canadian Journal of Earth Sciences* about two years after they visited Nuk Tessli. It was also covered in other media. The geologists concluded that the circle had been created by glacial movement.

Glacial ice is full of rocks and gravel, which are often carried many kilometres from their source. Large boulders deposited in this way are known as erratics, and the country is full of them. Having a foreign rock far divorced from its origin is therefore not unusual.

When fairly level sheets of ice melt, the sun can't penetrate surface rocks. The ice shrinks away around them but remains solid underneath. This eventually produces a mushroom formation with ice as the stalk and the rock as the cap. I have seen this myself; one glacier in Chile displayed dozens of them. Michael and Andrew maintained that a round, flat rock, thirty metres across, must have been thus balanced on an icy pedestal, then shattered, probably due to frost action. The pieces would gradually slide off to form the circle.

Given that there is no sign of similar rock beneath the circle, this seems to be the only explanation. I am still not convinced, however. The mushroom rocks that I observed in Chile were no more than three or four metres across and they were usually oval. The sun at colder latitudes never strikes the earth from overhead and the obliqueness of the angle causes uneven melting of the pedestal. When the rock becomes unbalanced, it falls off to one side. This happens regularly with the rock cairns I have built to mark trails.

If the geologists' theory is correct, the erratic that formed the Nuk Tessli stone circle must have been very thin and flat. If only a bit broke off at a time, the mushroom stem would shrink before another part was released, and the alien stones would be scattered all through the circle's centre. There isn't a single one in the middle. Therefore, as far as I could see, the rock must have shattered and fallen off all at once.

What would cause a round, thirty-metre-across flat boulder, sitting on a pedestal of ice, to break in an instant?

Perhaps it was hit by a meteor ...

The Flood

The 2010 winter had been a low-snow one, and the succeeding summer was hot and dry. The record-breaking pack and subsequent wet summer of 2007 might as well not have existed. Once more, fires sprang up all over the Chilcotin and the communities of Nimpo and Anahim lakes were again cut off by blazes on both sides of the top of the Hill and near Alexis Creek. It seemed as though fire was becoming a way of life. Toward the end of August, a wild windstorm was forecast, which, because there was no significant body of water between them, meant that the closest blaze near the top of the Hill was a possible danger to Anahim Lake. Everyone from Anahim Lake to Tatla Lake was told to evacuate, but with the road closed at both ends, where could they go? They wouldn't have had gas to go anywhere in any case because the gas trucks couldn't get through. Having no phone at Nuk Tessli, I knew about this only because Rosemary at the Precipice had emailed me.

My cabins were well south of the fire's potential path and I was not particularly worried about it. A change of wind that would point the fire in my direction would not be a concern, because it would then come from the north and lose its power. *Nuk tessli*, the southwest wind, was the only one to be feared. We even had less smoke than most that year, although we could often see it hanging in a thick brown cloud over Charlotte Lake.

When the storm came, the wind veered and drove the fire north of Anahim Lake. Within a few hours, the wind had died. The storm preceded a cold front; the temperature dropped about fifteen degrees Celsius. It brought a few spits of rain.

There was a pause. It was as if the weather gods were toying with us. More rain fell. And more. Suddenly, a switch had been flicked. All those years of drought and fires, and now the rain would not stop. It wasn't just a steady fall: each time it precipitated, it lasted for hours, and it poured.

September is normally a calm, sunny month with cool mornings and achingly clear days, but that year, we had dump after dump of rain. Some fell as a covering of wet, sticky snow at Nuk Tessli, but it soon melted around the cabins. I was a little surprised to see no increase in the lake level. There is over a metre's difference between high and low water, which makes it a nuisance to design docks and floats. The level is highest at breakup, and usually drops very quickly at the beginning of the season. Halfway through summer, the lake falls more gradually. If we get a couple of days' rain in September, the lake normally comes up a few centimetres. This year, despite all these downpours, it didn't. I was a little puzzled by this.

I was booked to fly out of Nuk Tessli shortly after my last clients of the season had left, on September 25. Once again, it was deluging; I had no way of knowing if the weather was the same at Nimpo, but as the plane didn't come, I assumed the pilot considered it too bad to fly. Stacked in my cabin were the dozens of boxes of stuff I wanted to take with me: personal items; recyclables; two laptops (I always packed an old one as a spare); satellite modems; a couple of boxes of office work that would need attention; journals; cameras and battery chargers (again, two of each); numerous other bits and pieces. There was nowhere dry to store them by the wharf.

The morning of the twenty-sixth dawned hazily sunny. As no one at Nimpo had sent me an email regarding weather conditions there, I would simply have to wait and see if anyone turned up. September mornings are often fogged in at Nimpo even if it is beautifully sunny at Nuk Tessli. When the plane arrived late in the morning, the pilot told me he had indeed needed to wait out the fog.

Because it looked as though the rain was going to hold off, I had started to pack the boxes down to the wharf not long after the sun came up. I like to have everything ready for a pilot when he comes, especially if he has been delayed by weather, for he might have a big lineup of clients. When I got to the wharf with the first load, I could not believe my eyes. The lake had risen forty-five centimetres overnight. The maximum rise I had ever recorded in such a short time period before was fifteen centimetres. The lake was almost as high as it normally was in spring. I immediately thought of Bella Coola. This Nuk Tessli watershed is one of several catchment areas that feed the Bella Coola River. The valley down there is long and narrow with steep, precipitous sides. Although people are discouraged from doing so, many live on the flood plain because there is nowhere else to go. For a couple of decades, they will get away with it. Floods have happened before down there, but this one, I found out later, was to go down in history as being the worst anyone could remember. All the rivers coming down the mountains blew out and destroyed the road in many different places. The stretch of Highway 20 that joins the top of the Hill to Bella Coola was closed for six weeks.

It wasn't just the Bella Coola watershed that went crazy. The turnoff to my winter place was closed by another river that went berserk. Six kilometres of highway were washed away on both sides of my turnoff, cutting me off. I managed to walk in, but having not been at Ginty Creek for four months, I had little food there and was evacuated to Nimpo where I had to stay for ten days.

When the river at Ginty Creek rose so dramatically, I wondered if there had been a blockage at higher elevations as had happened with Pandemonium Creek in 1937. But all the rivers had behaved in the same way. Apparently, when it rained throughout that September, the precipitation had fallen as snow higher in the mountains. I had seen a bit of whitening on the peaks around Nuk Tessli, but that is normal for September and it hadn't seemed excessive. It explained why my lake had not risen, though. The deluge on the twenty-fifth was accompanied by a dramatic rise in temperature, and all the snow melted at once. The unleashed fury of the water was mind-boggling.

I wasn't able to see if there had been any damage to Nuk Tessli until the following June. When I landed with the first plane of the season, the float and the wharf seemed fine. With some trepidation, I checked all the bridges. I have built six over the years. All the creeks could be crossed at low water, but were impassable for at least half of the summer. Some bridges were just a single log with a flattened top and a rope strung from trees doing duty as a hand rail. Others were grander and boasted two logs. Three of the bridges would need a hike to get to, but the others were where water ran into or out of the lake and could be reached by canoe. The one across the outlet of the lake, which had been my first as well as the biggest, was fine. Another small one was floating, as it usually was at the beginning of summer, but it was well held by ropes and would settle back into place as the lake level dropped. The third spanned the river where it came into the lake. It had been difficult to find a good place to secure it, and it had been dislodged before. It was still there, half buried under a waterfall, but no longer sitting on its foundations. I was expecting wwoofers soon, and levering it back into place would be one of the first jobs they would tackle.

The surprising thing, though, was the presence of a forty-four-gallon gas drum bobbing in the water on the far side of this bridge. It was a very old drum made of heavy steel; most of the original paint had flaked off years ago. I knew where it had come from. At the head of the lake above Nuk Tessli's the trapper had built a rough shack for a winter shelter. It had almost fallen into the ground. Round the back was a big pile of junk:

old snowmobile parts; bear-chewed plastic gas cans; coils of wire. Both the shack and the garbage pile were hidden from the lake. Only if you knew where to go would you see them.

It is difficult to carry gas on horseback. Horse's skin is sensitive to it and if the containers leak, the horse will be burned. So the trapper had his gas flown in to the lake. The water was very shallow near the cabin, and the gas had been stored on a little point about half a kilometre along the shore. The drums lay there, abandoned and half overgrown. They were an eyesore, and I had tried to move them to the trapper's garbage pile where they would be less visible, but they were too heavy. They must have been full of either water or gas or a mixture. I briefly thought of trying to drain them, but then all the contents would have run into the lake. I had no idea how diluted the contents were but did not want to risk any more contamination.

They had been sitting there for at least thirty years, but they had never budged. The fact that this flood had managed to dislodge one of them showed the lakes must have reached a record high after I had flown out. Gas is lighter than water, so even if the drum had been full, it would have floated. When the wwoofers came and fixed the bridge, they towed the drum home behind their canoe. We heaved it onto the wharf. It seemed to be about two thirds full. I undid the tap. It smelled pretty gassy but even if it had no water in it, it was so old I wouldn't have wanted to try to use it. A Beaver's door is designed to accommodate one of these drums. One time, when an empty plane was going out, I asked the pilot to take it to Nimpo, which he kindly did, and disposed of it.

The only other damage of note was another bridge about an hour's hike away from Nuk Tessli. It was crucial to the route to the road. It crossed the river that comes down from Wilderness Lake, where it flows out of what the trappers called Octopus Lake because of its many arms. In springtime, that river was impossible to wade. It was wide there, and mostly no more than knee deep, but for three paces there was a much deeper, faster flow, and the rocks on the bottom were extremely slippery. (I know because I tried crossing it on more than one occasion.) Eventually I found a place to bridge it. Octopus Lake was higher than Nuk Tessli so the trees were even scrubbier, and it was quite a problem finding any that were long enough to span the river. I built it in pre-wwoofer days. I packed a tent, food and tools—including the come-along, ropes and a chainsaw—to the site and spent a couple of days, mostly up to my waist in water, manhandling two logs across the channel.

It did good duty for many years, but the heavy spring runoff after the big snow in 2007 washed it clean away. The rope hand-rail still hung from the trees. In September of that year, I had two useful wwoofers who helped me build another bridge. The weather was hot and sunny, so dragging logs for several hundred metres through shallow water was not too onerous a job. The two wwoofers constructed a much more solid structure on tall rock pedestals. We wedged it with short logs on the downstream side and roped it to various trees upstream. I had hoped it would not go too far if the water was high again, but nothing could have prepared us for this flood. The ropes had stopped the logs from being washed away completely, but they were lopsided and wobbly and half-buried in water. Fortunately, five strong young men arrived at Nuk Tessli later in the summer. They were actually clients, and bridge building had not been what they were expect-ing, but within an afternoon, they had it reinstated.

Although the snow level had not been high during the winter after the flood, the ground was still absolutely saturated, and we had a very cool, wet summer. It rained every day until the middle of August. The BC Bird Breeding Atlas program was in full swing and two parties of birders came to Nuk Tessli. The second lot were more official and they were a fun bunch of guys. We would walk along for a while, take note of what we saw on route, then stop and listen intensely for five minutes. I'd thought I had been in tune with nature, especially when I walked alone, but those

Octopus Lake bridge.

five minutes of silent listening made me even more aware of my surroundings. I often rested during my hikes, of course, and generally registered bird calls as I moved, but I rarely concentrated on that single sense. It was an interesting experience and I vowed to do it more often.

We hiked in many directions but it was difficult to observe many of the species properly because in wind and rain birds don't waste their energy singing. One man was particularly interested in grouse and ptarmigan, and I took the group to a spot where I often heard and sometimes saw blue grouse booming. The noise is similar to that created when someone blows across the top of a bottle. But that day it was as if the blue grouse did not exist.

On the whole I didn't mind the wet too much: I'd had such a long run of worry about fires that it was a relief to have a summer free of them. The rain and high water produced a heavy bug year, but otherwise, the flood had made very little impact. There were small areas of damage along some of the rivers that made me wish I had been able to see the water at its peak of power, but that was it.

Interim

I hear a plane. Earlier, a Cessna buzzed overhead, but it had been too high and coming from the wrong direction to be my intended visitor; in any case I knew he would be arriving with a Beaver. Now a deeper note drones distantly like a tired fly against a window pane. It is low, coming from the north. This will be the person I am expecting. Surprisingly, he is arriving pretty much when he said he would.

It will take a while for the plane to land, turn and taxi to the wharf, but already I am getting to my feet and beginning to walk down the rocky trail to the waterfront. The Beaver is seen only briefly as it wobbles over the ridge at the foot of the lake, then it is hidden again as it dips behind Big Island. When it emerges, the floats are already touching the water, spewing twin white fountains behind them. The friendly breeze slows the plane quickly, but it has overshot the channel between the islands: occasionally pilots will touch down soon enough to turn without extra taxiing. I remember one guy swinging into the channel on a single float, but his plane was empty. This Beaver will be loaded with freight—in fact, I can see lumber strapped to the float struts. Pilots must naturally be more cautious when they are carrying external cargo. All of the pre-sawn lumber I used at Nuk Tessli arrived either inside or strapped to the outside of visitors' planes.

Beaver floatplane at Nuk Tessli's wharf.

The Beaver is turning. It is heading slowly toward the channel, bobbing a little on the waves it created when it landed. As it comes toward the wharf, the sun is behind it; the windows are dark and I can see nothing of the people inside. I am not even sure who the pilot will be. Sometimes I can tell by the way they fly in: each has a preferred angle and height that he favours. All I know is that it must be someone familiar with the territory, for a pilot new to the lake would come in higher and make a flyover first to check it out.

I also do not know how many passengers there will be. At one time the man who is arriving told me he might be bringing friends. I am always apprehensive when a plane is bringing strangers. If I take a dislike to someone, it is hard for me to be civil. I put a smile on my face anyway. I may not be able to see them, but they will have a clear view of me. Almost everyone takes pictures when they are approaching the wharf. I owe them a smile, at least, to begin with.

The motor is switched off and the plane swings so that it can approach the wharf side-on. The pilot jumps onto his float and grabs a rope that is fastened by one end to a strut. Another, smaller rope hangs from the wing, and it is this I catch, but most pilots don't need the extra help. Mine is a tricky wharf, though, for the last metre or two is suddenly sheltered and it is easy to overshoot and career into the rocky shore.

This pilot has timed it well. He had put his water rudders at exactly the right angle to bring the plane alongside; he leaps onto my wharf and snags his rope around a cleat. There is only one passenger—the friends must not have been able to make it. He is already climbing out of his side of the plane. I have met him before. He stayed at Nuk Tessli for a few days a couple of years ago. He is very excited: "Hullo, Chris!" he sings. I make myself look calm and happy. "Welcome to Nuk Tessli," I say.

Another door in my existential journey has been opened. It is one that I built myself, but it is going to be very difficult for me to pass through it.

The Sale

The money that I had inherited, and which I had used to buy and start building at Ginty Creek, was obviously not going to be enough to complete my dream. When I first moved onto the property, I erected a small cabin in a hurry, but planned a much more salubrious home. All my adult life I'd lived out of backpacks, in tents and in houses lacking many facilities such as electricity or piped water, and now I felt it was time to indulge in a few luxuries. I wanted running water and, if I could swing it, I might even have grid power as well. The house would have an attic and a basement and a shop. There would be a small guest cabin for wwoofers and friends, which would double as a little gallery for unsold books and artwork, and also as a storage place for the projector, lights and display units and other paraphernalia of a slide show tour. These were squeezed into the little cabin's attic right now, and were a pain to haul up and down the narrow steps.

I had now built five cabins: the first one at Lonesome Lake, three at Nuk Tessli and the new one at Ginty Creek. The construction of these had been spread over a quarter of a century, but each had taken two or three years to finish. In other words, I had spent a good part of my adult life building. I have never liked doing it. But it was the only way I knew how to get what I wanted. The thought of tackling building number six was overwhelmingly depressing, and it was going to cost quite a bit of money. Even if I did most of the work myself, there were virtually no trees suitable for building at Ginty Creek, and almost all materials would have to be bought. How was I going to finance it?

The Ginty Creek property comprised two titles. They were surrounded by Crown land on three sides; the fourth side ran along a river. Across the river was a small ranch. Though my neighbours had become quiet and pleasant people after their initial noisy start (screaming snowmobiles, shooting guns, etc.), I had a hard time dealing with anyone who lived so close. At Nuk Tessli I was used to hearing no other human noise except a few light aircraft, and most of those would be coming to visit me. It was as if I were queen of a vast, unpopulated realm. I knew of almost every human being that set foot in the place, except for a few of the fliers who landed on other lakes and rarely left the vicinity of their planes. I was also familiar with the habits of many of the four-legged travellers, too. The sense of freedom of spirit that is manifested by being mentally and spiritually connected to such a large realm is very difficult to describe to people who never have been, and cannot imagine being, alone. So to have other human beings within sight and earshot, with their barking dogs and ATVs and chainsaws and pumps and tractors, was a constant source of irritation to me, particularly as the dominant wind blew the noise toward me. Until I bought Ginty Creek, I had always spent at least three months of the winter at Nuk Tessli, longer if I stayed through breakup. During the first months at Ginty Creek the neighbours' noises pierced my soul, and I was very homesick for the mountains.

I was now in my seventh decade and trying to come to grips with the acknowledgement that I was no longer immortal. My health was very good for the most part, but I had fibromyalgia, and arthritis in both knees, which meant I had to deal with a certain level of chronic pain and was having to slow down. Getting a paying job, even if I could tolerate it, would not have been very lucrative because I would have had to use a good chunk of the income for accommodation—there was certainly no work to be had within driving distance. Finding the right place to live would be further complicated by having two large, very much outdoor dogs. To get the money to build my dream home, I decided that I would have to sell one of the Ginty Creek properties: the one on the river, closest to the neighbours. I didn't like the idea of having people living even nearer than they already were. The cabin I had built was half a kilometre away from my dream home—a great distance for a city dweller, but for someone used to a lot of space, this is hard to accept. Like most people in this world, however, I was going to have to compromise. If I sold the river property maybe I could even afford to hire someone to do the building and save me that onerous chore as well. For a while, I had the idea of trading the lower property to someone who would build my dream home on the upper one. That would take care of both nasty problems. A couple of parties were vaguely interested, and this idea dragged on for a year or two, but it soon became obvious that it was not going to work.

In the meantime, the property across the river was sold twice within ten months. The newest new owners decided to go into the Arctic for a couple of years to earn money to finish paying for it. They had no animals so would not need caretakers. A few days after they left, I walked beside the river. The emptiness of the property across the water was liberating. I found myself relaxing in a way I had yet to do at Ginty Creek. Even though I would never walk on the property—the wild waters of the river were rarely safe to cross—just knowing it was untenanted allowed my soul to expand. I realized that I would be crazy to sell or trade the river property, but what was I going to do for money? A thought suddenly popped into the forefront of my mind. It was Nuk Tessli that was going to have to go.

I suppose the idea had been chugging around my brain cells for a while. Because of the aches and pains, it was difficult for me to keep up with many of the clients. I would guide them to a lookout (sensing their frustration at my slowness every step of the way), point out their options, make sure they knew how to pick up the trail again, then follow them down at my own speed. I could still cover the ground reasonably well and enjoy hikes and flowers, but not at the pace most clients preferred.

Summers at Nuk Tessli were becoming increasingly full of people. At the beginning and end of the season I would have wwoofers, and in the middle would come the clients. Friends also visited sometimes. Occasionally these parties would overlap, but on the whole I found it easier not to mix them. Apart from the overcrowding that would ensue, I found it difficult to think in different mental directions at the same time. When I wintered at Nuk Tessli, I had lots of time to enjoy the place alone; because I was now there only in the summer, I seemed to spend all my time either dealing with people or recovering from them, and I had little energy for my own explorations. Nuk Tessli was becoming work.

Having the idea of parting with Nuk Tessli on the back burner was one thing, but actually bringing it to the fore was a whole different ball game. I had created a wonderful place for myself from nothing—not just a shelter, but a lifestyle encompassing my love of wilderness and writing. Even if I didn't think it was particularly unusual, I was proud of my achievement, and since everyone continuously asked me why I had done it, I had grown to enjoy being thought eccentric. (I am not eccentric, of course: I am simply not city. No one who lives out here thinks what I have done strange at all.)

Nuk Tessli had become the way everyone thought of me, and I liked it. Never mind that Ginty Creek was still wilderness by most people's definition, being without radio signal, running water or anything but home-made power. Never mind that it was three and a half hours' drive (in good weather) from the nearest bank, cellphone frequency or supermarket. Ginty Creek had a road (albeit a rough one). It was accessible. If I parted with Nuk Tessli I would not be just disposing of a business and changing the view: I would be selling a way of life.

In March of 2009, I listed Nuk Tessli on a couple of For Sale By Owner websites. Because it was situated on a backcountry recreation Crown lease, there were some restrictions to the sale. No one could buy the land; they could only buy the buildings and the cabins. They would also have to continue to run a tourist business in some form or other, and would have to negotiate with the government for the lease. At least one of the new owners had to be a Canadian citizen or BC resident.

A prospective buyer would naturally want to know about the profits and losses over the years and this would be a real drawback to the sale, because, despite the buildup of publicity, both through books and slide show tours, the business had never made a profit. Just when I started to get more clients, the government put up their fees exponentially. Some years I would finish a few thousand ahead, but it was always a situation of one financial step forward and two back. In all my time there, the place just about broke even. If I hadn't had the extra income from my books, minimal though it was, I would not have been able to eat. I did not mind this for myself—I would not have changed the life I had created for anything—but as a selling point, it was disastrous.

I didn't expect Nuk Tessli to be snapped up immediately. It was a depressed time financially in British Columbia. Half the Chilcotin was for sale. Notices, some commercial-looking real estate signs and some crudely home-made, seemed to decorate every other driveway. And Nuk Tessli was a very specialized place. I had come to realize that the logistics of getting there and organizing supplies required a different way of thinking from what most people were used to. I figured it might take a year or two for the sale to go ahead. I still had a little money and could start building my dream house. The book tours brought in a few thousand a year; Nuk Tessli would continue to pay for itself. Like I have done for most of my life, I would keep spending and hope for the best.

I started receiving inquiries regarding the sale right away, but despite my efforts to explain everything on the websites, most people obviously didn't have a clue. One lady phoned me and asked if I thought it would make a suitable retirement home for cats and dogs. I expect it would: the elderly critters would be gleefully welcomed, no doubt, by the bears. Another man worked for a Texas oil company and needed to relocate to Canada. The house "had to be suitable for a business executive." A couple from Vancouver showed some suitability. I even met them during the winter before they came in. They were naturalists and hikers, and planned to fight their way in from the road in July. Nuk Tessli's trails are not marked on any maps. Since I no longer hiked in myself, the original trail that I had brushed out had grown over again. The *BC Backroads Mapbook* published a spider's web of dashed and dotted lines supposedly representing trails in the area, but these were either hopelessly overgrown or in the wrong place, or they did not exist. After three parties tried to use this book to hike into the area I contacted the publisher and they have now changed the information.

If people want to hike in to Nuk Tessli, I tell them that the best way for them to have accurate information is to send me the two relevant topo maps; I will draw the route and indicate which features to look for on them before mailing them back. I warn everyone that I rarely receive mail more than once or twice a month so this will take time.

The wannabe buyers who planned to hike in had been given this information when I met them in February. I also told them that the *BC Backroads Mapbook* of that time was useless. About three days before they were due to leave Vancouver, they emailed me a couple of pages scanned from the book and asked me to confirm that the routes were accurate. I replied frantically that these were wrong, but it was impossible to explain things properly over the Internet. Instead of a single overnight hike, they took four days. Part of this was because they were birding, but a lot was because they had never hiked in rough country before. Bushwhacking bears no resemblance to walking on graded footpaths. They ignored my instructions to stay beside the water in the narrow valley on the Charlotte Lake side of the trip, tried to go higher and ended up in terrible rocks and brush and windfall where the man had quite a bad fall. They finally made it to Nuk Tessli wet, exhausted and severely bitten.

The first thing one of them said to me was, "We love it but we really don't have the money." Didn't they know they had no money before we started all this? I had expended a considerable amount of time and emotional energy trying to help them, as well as sending all the usual information—Land Office restrictions, Google maps, cabins, income and expenditure. It was a lesson learned for me. I asked the next inquirer up front if he could finance it as I didn't want to go through the process for nothing again. He could, and he seemed a pleasant, straightforward person, but he was looking for something closer to a city where he could take people on day hikes. I guess these frustrations are how real estate agents earn their money.

The inquiries kept coming but all were totally off the wall. I renewed the listing for a second year, and then a third. A couple of retirement age flew in for a few hours on a perfect September day. The man was a mechanic and good with his hands; the woman apparently enjoyed cooking. They thought they might open a B & B. Did they think people were just going to drop in? They had obviously no idea what running a place like Nuk Tessli was all about. It's the advertising, organizing of supplies months in advance, being on duty twenty-four hours a day, sacrificing one's own pleasures for others, the difficulty of bending all activities to the weather. They told me they were going to make an offer, but first, they would have to talk to the bank about getting a loan. I could have told them that no bank was going to hand out a loan on a Crown lease that did not make a profit. They contacted me a couple of weeks later quite surprised to confess that the loan was not forthcoming. Once again a lot of emotional effort on my part came to nothing.

One man, whom I shall refer to as Red, had started a tourist business in British Columbia a few years before, but had no base. We talked for a while and he seemed very pleasant. I offered him the use of Nuk Tessli for some of his trips; he could guide the more energetic people, and I would take the plodders. Everyone I knew who had dealt with him said he was charming and handled people very well.

Next thing, an article in a prominent outdoor magazine stated that the famous Chris Czajkowski of Nuk Tessli was retiring and *handing over the keys* to Red. The magazine never contacted me: I was informed of the article by a friend. I was livid. A prospective buyer I was negotiating with found out and was incensed. Was I going behind his back? I phoned the magazine at once and the editor was immediately contrite—he had thought Red's words were true. He vowed to make a public apology but it was a month before the next edition came out. Red seemed amazed that I would be angry. Of course he had to exaggerate his image; otherwise he could not sell his product. I had to write to him several times before he deleted Nuk Tessli from his website. What jerks there are in this world.

Another couple who seemed quite promising popped into the picture. They had guided wilderness clients for twenty years in Alaska. They wanted to relocate farther south. They were obviously experienced with mixing tourists and wild country, and they told me they had just sold a house and therefore had the money. When they met me at Ginty Creek not long after I had flown out of the mountains one year, they told me they had three boys aged five to twelve. Whereas the boys were great in the bush, they added, they felt they needed a place that could give the kids more social life than would be possible at Nuk Tessli. Quite understandable, but why go through this process when they knew this before they came? They then asked me if they could rent the Nuk Tessli cabins for the winter. Under other circumstances I might have agreed, but what if they burned one of them down? I had never been able to afford fire insurance, and if the cabins were destroyed, I would have nothing left to sell. The winter's rent they offered me was pathetic. Either property was worth a lot less in Alaska or the couple was really naïve. In the end I came to the conclusion that they never had any intention of making a serious offer; they had just wanted a cheap place to have fun for the winter.

The oddest query was from a man calling himself Mick Papoudopolus. He had a UK email address, but his English was so bad it was difficult to understand. He contacted me via the For Sale By Owner website. I have reproduced his correspondence as he wrote it.

August 8, 2011
Hello Chris,

How are you doing and how was the weekend? I am so much interested in this, please give me more information on it.
  Thanks and i await your mail.
  Mick

I sent him the usual blurb, emphasizing that the land could not be bought, that the property had to be run as a commercial business and could not be kept for private use and that at least one of the partners (if any) who bought it had to be a Canadian resident or citizen. I also explained something about the logistics of getting there: fly from Vancouver on the three-days-a-week schedule, get picked up by the float plane company and taken to the float plane base twenty kilometres away, then fly to Nuk Tessli. Bring your own sleeping bag. A few days later I received the following, which was obviously copied to someone called David.

August 11, 2011

Hello Chris,
> *Am sorry for the late reply, am still so much inter-ested in it.*
> *Hello David*
> *I received your email and its quite noble of you. With what you have said about the house i am so much interested in it.*
> *I will contact my Financial Adviser as regards the finalization of this property. I will also like to know if the property's price is negotiable so please state in your email your final price as I will not want to get in to any form of money miss-cordiality.*
> *Final Price —*
> *I will call you Asap if need be and I will also have my Account Officer call you to conclude of mode of payment so I will get back to you after you next reply so I will know the necessary things you will have to do if any. After finalizing the process i will come over to check it out.*
> *Please also send me your phone number.*
> *Mick*

I had the place listed for $175,000, but said I was prepared to negotiate. I told him I had no phone up in the mountains. I asked him what business he operated in England and whether or not he would have time to run a tourist resort in Canada.

August 12, 2011

Hello,
> *Thanks for the mail..*
> *I can pay you 150,000 US$*
> *I just want to ask if there is a montage on the property.*
> *But I am going to have problem because i can't get you on phone and am not ok with that.*
> *I am the owner of Techview Construction company here in UK.*
> *www.techviewconstruction.org.*
> *Thanks so much for the mail and i await your mail..*
> *Mick*

I at once looked up the website. At first glance, it was impressive. Three large photos filled the home page: road construction in Africa, a large highway bridge and some kind of tall, modern building. But there was very little other information. On "About Us" there was a portrait of a striking man in his forties, movie-star handsome but with black, slicked-back hair in a style fifty years out of date. I clicked on "Gallery" and up popped a message that the page was under construction. A British mailing address and phone number were listed.

That evening I received another email:

August 12, 2011

Good Day,
> *Thanks so much for the mail. I am ok with everything you have said. I will pay the 150.000 US$ is that ok by you? Yes, that is my picture and am from Greece. I have been to Russia so many time so i am use to the cold weather. Also ruining both is not a problem. I will*

have to make the payment before coming over because
i don't want to lose that place and also i will be living
UK for Germany soon due to business so when am back
i will come over with my wife to check it out. But i will
really love to pay before living for Germany.
So how is the mode of payment? Do you have equity
line of credit account?
Thanks so much and do get back to me
God Bless you and Greetings from family to you..
Mick

I didn't know what an equity line of credit account was. I might not be very savvy in the financial world but thought this whole business very fishy. I wrote to a friend who knew quite a bit more about finances than I did. He replied:

Hi Chris.
This one smells really bad to me. The website is sus-
picious and very flimsy—in fact it tells you nothing …
You would almost certainly be unable to get a "home
equity line of credit" as a bank would not issue you one
in case you defaulted on the loan. I am concerned that
he is asking about it as a way to buy your property by
making payments over a time … he may be seeing this
as a way to get access to your credit card to do this …
It could well be that he is trying to launder money, or
possibly simply move money out of Greece to avoid taxes
as the financial situation there is precarious at this time.
I think if you state firmly your intentions he will
simply melt away.

Even without that advice, I would never have sold Nuk Tessli sight unseen. Canadians had a hard time understanding the logistics of the place; I did not see how a Greek with an imperfect understanding of English could ever comprehend. I wrote and told Mick that I couldn't accept the money until after he had seen the place and never heard from him again. And, in case you are wondering, within a few days, the website ceased to exist!

Apparently, money launderers often cruise real estate sites. I told the above story to some Nuk Tessli visitors, two of whom were from Spain. One was a real estate lawyer. She said a colleague was handling the sale of a property in Paris. It was, perforce, worth a considerable amount of money. She went with the seller to meet a prospective purchaser at a coffee shop nearby. The buyer was prepared to sign the papers at once: he would have paid the full amount instantly. He had the cash in a suitcase with him.

Doron

Not long after I first listed the place, a man spoke to me on the telephone (it was during the spring and I was still at Ginty Creek). He asked many questions. There was no paperwork or contact by email and I forgot about him. The following August I received an email. The subject line was gobbledygook, a collection of symbols similar to what people sometimes write to indicate swearing. It was the kind of thing one would normally delete unread, but a bit of the message was visible and I took the risk of opening it. It was aligned to the right. Again, I have used the original spelling.

Hi
I am looking for a wilderness property in BC and came across your place.
Can you please give same more information?
Is it privet land? How big is the land?
Is it possible to get to the place overland by horse beck or snowmachin?
Are there any taxes on the property?
Thank
You very much
Doron Erel.

Under his name was a website ending in .il. I clicked on it and the alphabet was like none I had ever seen before. The only thing I could read was a heading that said *English,* and I clicked on it and found that Doron was from Israel. He was the first person from his country to climb Everest and the first to go to Antarctica; he had kayaked near Greenland and guided hikers in the Himalayas, European Alps and Alaska.

I explained that it was impossible to buy the land, told him the average annual costs (rent, taxes, compulsory insurance, head tax, etc.) and also tried to explain the difficulties of using horses (which could get to within a couple of kilometres, otherwise it was too rocky) and snowmobiles, which required considerable experience as the lower country would be tangled with windfall, snow in the lee of ridges would be deep and soft, and all water had to be treated with the greatest of caution. Only the middle of large lakes during the coldest parts of the year could be trusted without good, local knowledge. I also said that Nuk Tessli might seem tame after his impressive exploits but he replied that of all the places he'd visited, he liked the Pacific Northwest best.

We exchanged more emails. I described the hike in, the weather, the wildlife, the fishing, the number of visitors a year (lots, but not many paying guests!). He told me his wife and three sons were Canadian, and asked me about electricity (very small solar power system to run the laptop and satellite Internet), warm water (in a kettle on the stove), showers (a plastic bag heated up in the sun—you could be creative and heat water on the stove for that, too) and toilets (outhouse!). He informed me that he would be in Alaska at the end of September and would fit in a trip to Nuk Tessli afterwards. I had not planned on staying in the mountains so late, so Doron rearranged his schedule to come to my place before his Alaskan venture. He wanted to make sure I would not sell the place before he arrived. Fat chance of that.

He would come here directly from Tel Aviv and would arrive in Williams Lake on the evening of September 8, after being "twenty hours in the sky." He would rent a truck so that he could visit other properties in the area, and would fly to Nuk Tessli on the ninth, bringing fresh food for dinner. I never asked him to bring anything; his offer indicated he was familiar with the logistics of living so far from stores. He obviously knew how difficult it was to organize fresh food in a place like this. He expected to stay for five days.

After a hot, sunny August, we suddenly had chilly weather with some half-hearted rain. A Cessna dodged in under the overcast and hopped over the ridge at the foot of the lake. Doron was medium-sized and wiry. He had a ready smile and made himself instantly at home by marching over to the wood heater and starting to cook. He popped the hot stove door open with a bit of wood, shoved more fuel in, and banged the door shut with bare fingers— the marks of someone very used to wilderness cooking. Volunteers who stay for a month rarely gain such dexterity with hot stove doors. He had brought a couple of exotic items: what appeared to be tahini (the label was all in Hebrew) and a spicy sauce.

I knew at once that I would never be able to keep up with Doron on a hike. I equipped him with my home-drawn trail map and pointed him toward the Lookout and the Mammaries. I suggested that on day two he might like to go up to Wilderness Lake and check out the cabin there. It belonged to another resort but I had occasionally incorporated it into a hut-to-hut hiking tour.

The hike I had shown Doron would have taken me all day but he was back within a few hours. The weather had remained poor and I thought he had maybe cut his trip short because of that, but he'd covered all the ground, which was impressive. Despite the weather, he admitted to seeing the potential of the place; however, he decided he could not justify spending so much money, and he asked me if I could contact the float plane base and book a flight out earlier than planned. That would give him more time to check out the properties for sale in the Bella Coola Valley. His knowledge of local real estate for sale far exceeded mine; he had information on every piece of land that was going in western North America. "But keep me informed," he said as he stepped into the plane.

. . . .

Life went on. Doron and I corresponded in a desultory way and a few months later he made me an offer—for a third of the asking price. This was not acceptable. At that time I had a couple of other prospective buyers who looked quite promising hovering in the wings. When these proved to be non-events, more cropped up. The sale was consuming my life. Each possible purchaser filled me with great hope, and each failure dropped me down with a crash. I was on a roller coaster ride—up, then down; up, then down.

I was now getting very short of money, to the point where I was going into debt, a "civilized" aspect of life I have never been able to handle. Probably because I have never had a guaranteed income. I was also finding that trying to run two properties, both my winter home and the mountain business, was too much for me. Many people think running a resort is just a question of sitting on the deck and going fishing, but it is a highly stressful 24/7 occupation, even when you can drive in. If visitors to Nuk Tessli found everything running smoothly it was because I had already gone through all the headaches and angst. Now that I had decided to sell the place I really did not want to run it anymore.

A year after his visit, Doron made another offer. The problem was, I had no real idea of what the place was worth. The lease was so structured that I had to pay taxes as well as rent. One year, after a completely unexpected rent hike from one thousand to five thousand dollars, I went to the Land Office to query it, and they said that there was nothing quite like my place—no one could go into the bush and build off-road on Crown land now unless they were affiliated to a resort that had public road access. So, the guy at the desk told me, they made up the rules for Nuk Tessli as they went along.

A resort on a similar lease in the next valley, but much lower in altitude, was for sale: the owners were asking $430,000. This resort had more cabins and also boats and motors, but it had not been operational for several years and was very dirty and rundown. The assessed value for Nuk Tessli was $83,000, but that was for the land alone and didn't include all the work I had put into the place: the buildings, the trails, the publicity and so on. The outfitter who had title to the hunting rights around my property was also trying to sell. He was asking $200,000. His lease covered a larger area but he had no buildings at all, only temporary camps. Many of the pilots who came by said that Nuk Tessli was by far the most beautiful place they flew into. It had of course been chosen for the view. I had not wanted a lake suitable for sports fishing.

Doron's offer was still very low. After some negotiation, he crept up a bit. I suddenly thought, "What the heck! I need to get on with the rest of my life." All the other inquiries, perhaps forty of them, had fallen through due to the total unsuitability of the intended purchasers. The North American push-button culture is really so divorced from reality. Water, food, power and shelter are taken for granted. This bears no relationship to a life where one has to arrange these things for oneself. No wonder people keep asking me why I live this way. They simply cannot comprehend any other existence than one organized for them. Doron had so far proved to be the only prospective buyer who was anywhere near the same wavelength as I was. I might wait years before a better offer came along.

The winter months were filled with negotiating the method of payment and dealing with the Land Office. Doron is like me: he doesn't find his way easily around bureaucracy and it was a struggle for both of us to sort out what we needed to do. Doron's spoken English is good but, as I was to find with all the Israelis I eventually met, reading and writing were difficult, partly because the alphabet is so different, and partly because Hebrew is read from right to left. Suzan, Doron's wife, was Canadian-born and a lawyer to boot, but she had no experience with these kinds of documents and in any case was working full-time.

The biggest hurdle we had to overcome was a First Nations review. That had not been necessary when I had started Nuk Tessli, but it apparently had been done, without my knowledge, the last two times I had renewed the lease. Because a new owner was involved, however, we would have to wait two or three months to see if Doron's proposal was accepted.

A resort owner at Nimpo who was trying to sell a remote cabin with the same kind of lease was also going through a First Nations review. He was having all sorts of trouble and the process was taking months. If the review was not successful, the Land Office informed us, the sale could not go through. And yet big businesses, even if their industrial proposals are rejected all the way up to the supreme court, usually get around it eventually. Money overrides everything. Waiting for the review result was naturally a time of great anxiety for both Doron and myself. We couldn't approach a specific First Nation and find out what was going on as apparently several Band territories overlapped in the mountains.

Ginty Creek was a forty-minute drive from the post office so I didn't usually pick up mail more than two or three times a month. One day, a single-page document from the Land Office lay in my mail box. It was a copy of a cover letter sent to Doron's son, Sela, who was partnering Doron in the business, saying that since the First Nations review was successful, the enclosed forms should be signed and returned by the end of March. If the documents were not returned within that time, the application would be cancelled. The date given was only four days away.

My piece of mail contained only the cover letter, not the other documents. Sela was working in Alberta. I immediately emailed him, and Doron and Suzan, describing the cover letter and asking if any of them had received the Land Office's package. I also phoned the Land Office: they had apparently sent the documents to Sela two weeks before. It never fails to amaze me how government offices always assume that rural mail will reach its destination as quickly as it does in the city. I have often picked up a bill that is already overdue. Mail on Highway 20 comes only three times a week, and many people like myself don't go to the post office every mail day.

Sela had never received the Land Office letter; by pure chance he was planning to set off to visit me the day after I emailed him. I got the Land Office to send me the documents by email, and within twenty-four hours of Sela's arrival at Ginty Creek, we were able to organize the compulsory insurance, the business plan and the signing over of the lease. This last piece of paper suddenly brought it home to me. Previously Doron, Sela and I had agreed on a purchase plan, and I had received some of the money, with strict instructions that I couldn't yet spend it. Relinquishing the lease, however, made it final. I hadn't realized that, until this moment, I had still felt a modicum of control over the situation. With a lurch of my heart, I wrote my name. Nuk Tessli was no longer mine.

It had been agreed that I would go to Nuk Tessli for a couple of months that summer, partly to help Doron and Sela with the transition, but also because I had booked clients before the sale had taken place, and they had wanted to come while I was still there. I wasn't sure how I felt about sharing my time in the mountains. On the one hand it would be nice for me to be able to say goodbye to the place; on the other, having never had great skills as a people person, and having been used to being Queen of my Queendom, I would now have to deal with someone who was, in essence, my boss.

The Last Summer

For some reason, the ice went out extremely late in 2012. There was no excessive snow or cold, but April and May had temperatures well below average and Nuk Tessli stayed frozen even longer than it had done after the big snow year of 2007. Nimpo Lake also broke all remembered breakup records.

Once again I had to deal with the angst of flying. Even if it had been possible to trudge through the snow, I now found walking any distance quite painful. That spring I had been advised to have a knee replacement.

Flying was not the only problem I had to deal with at the beginning of that season. Doron was guiding canoeists in Alaska—again, this was pre-booked—so he could not arrive at Nuk Tessli until the end of June. Sela was embroiled in exams and would be coming later. Consequently I agreed to do all the basic shopping for the year. As always, I had made a list of food that remained in the attic before I left in the fall so I had a better idea of what would be needed. Fortunately, I wouldn't have to pay for it! I also told Doron that if I had room in my van I could bring building supplies. It turned out I had major problems with my van that spring, so I ended up driving into Williams Lake more frequently than usual and could bring quite a lot of stuff back with me. Fibreglass insulation was a big item. Doron planned on lining the attics for extra sleeping spaces and making insulated rooms

Tweedsmuir Air dock at Nimpo Lake.

for toilets and showers, which I thought unnecessary. "But we are used to hot climates," Doron said. "I thought you were tough, going to Everest and Antarctica," I countered with a smile.

But these things were now Doron's choice. Even when I had no room inside my van, I could tie bales of insulation onto the roof. It made it very easy to find my vehicle in the supermarket parking lot. I took everything to the float plane base, labelled it and stacked it in the hangar, ready to be flown in whenever there was plane space. Doron would purchase a vehicle and also shop on his way through. I strongly expected—and this proved to be the case—that Doron would want a number of items neither of us had thought of and would likely fly back out to Williams Lake at different times during the summer.

Because it was such a late year, I could not fly in until June 14. When the local pilots told me the lake was open, I booked a flight and drove to the wharf. I would hire a Beaver (what luxury to not have to pay for it!) and go through the usual hassle of trying to decide which were the most important items to take. I and my two dogs would use up about 120 kilograms of the freight allowance, and also the equivalent of two seats. Fortunately the dogs got on very well and could tolerate being jammed in a very small space. As another bonus, both these two were good fliers and I never had to worry about them in the air.

All the rear seats were removed and perishables like produce and some construction items were loaded. Even though they might not have been the most urgent, I packed a number of small items, worried that they might get lost, for other clients' equipment was stored in the hangar. Dried food that we couldn't get into the plane would stay in my van in the float plane company's yard. The van was looking pretty beat up by this time but as far as I knew, it was still mouseproof. Over the years, the float plane companies have been great at bringing in stuff whenever possible; much of their work involves lugging heavy and awkward items into and out of planes. You need a strong back: having that little gap between a wharf and the cabin of the plane makes slinging loads back and forth quite difficult.

Everything was loaded, including the dogs. A quick trip to the outhouse, a deep mental breath, and I was climbing the ladder, then sliding over the pilot's seat to reach my cramped place. I always had to let out the seat belts—seems as though everyone else who sat there was a lot skinnier than me. The radio headset was hung on a hook beside my head and I pulled it on.

I have had my share of bad weather flights, but on this occasion, the gods were smiling. Flying conditions could not have been more perfect: brilliant sun, clear blue sky and a tiny breeze to ruffle the water. Snow-laden peaks are visible from the float plane base, but these are not the bigger mountains that can be seen from my cabins; we would fly over these foothills to reach Nuk Tessli. Straight in front of us was Halfway Mountain. When I used to hike in from the end of the road, it was midway on my journey. Every time I look at it I imagine myself picking a way through the tundra around its shoulder and enjoying the panoramic view, the lake nestled within its ring of mountains and the scattering of wildflowers colouring the meadows at my feet.

We taxied far into the lake so we could turn into the wind, which was coming from the north. The Beaver makes a terrific racket when it takes off: the propeller blades actually break the sound barrier. At first we hardly moved. The plane sat heavily in the water and threw up a mighty wave. It seemed as though nothing could part us from this watery embrace. Then we got onto the step, where only the bottom of the floats is touching the lake. If it is very calm, the pilot may need to rock the plane to get one of the floats free, but with a nice little breeze, liftoff was smooth.

We swung round toward the mountains. Halfway there we crossed Charlotte Lake, at the east end of which is the cabin the trapping family used to use as a winter base. That is also where I left my vehicle when I hiked or snowshoed in. Our flight route took us over the other end of the lake, several kilometres away. A gaggle of summer cabins and mansions litter the north side of the lake and we flew directly over these. They are linked by an unplanned tangle of dusty roads winding through the scrubby, beetle-killed pines. I often wondered if they knew that it was me flying overhead. Flightseeing tours pass this way, but they are on the return trip to Nimpo when they cross Charlotte Lake, and they would be going in the other direction.

All my dogs have dealt with flying differently. Some hated it; one, the biggest I had, would cry the whole way. It was a terrible fight to get him inside. Badger and Harry are my current companions; both are complacent. Harry always curls up in the tiny space allowed him and goes to sleep. Badger, however, sits and looks out the window, seemingly with great interest. What he could possibly see up there beats me.

The holiday cabins were the last sign of habitation that we saw, although the marks of man continue a bit longer. South of the lake,

Badger in the plane.

the fire roads built for the 2004 Lonesome Lake fire are still much in evidence. After some argument by those of us who wanted to keep the wild country as pristine as possible, Cats were put back in there to pull the bulldozed trees onto the road again. People were driving along them and chainsawing their own trails into the bush. Even during the fire, people were defying the evacuation order, cutting their way to the abandoned resorts and stealing fishing equipment. Roads are the scourge of wild country. Logging looks messy, but if cutblocks are left alone long enough, the land will eventually heal itself. Once machines get in there on a regular basis, wilderness is doomed. Water is polluted; garbage is strewn; plants and soil are eroded and everything moving is shot.

We crossed the fire roads and entered the narrow river valley that houses one branch of Whitton Creek. Low peaks rise on either side. This is where it usually starts to get bumpier; on this day, there were a few little wriggles but nothing too nerve-wracking. We droned over a couple of skinny lakes. The small mountains on either side grew higher and snowier. Goats lived on these slopes but were impossible to pick out in the snow. We hopped over the last steep ridge, and Nuk Tessli was spread before us—the deep blue lake, the blinding white mountains, the thick, dark pelt of bush and the square point jutting into the lake where the cabins stood.

Although it had been an easy winter as far as cold and snow levels were concerned, we had been plagued by strong, wild winds. At Ginty Creek I never went anywhere in the vehicle without taking a chainsaw as I would almost always have to cut a tree off the road. Nuk Tessli was no stranger to maniacal winds, and every time I flew in my first concern was whether or not the cabins still had a roof. They seemed to be on as we sped by in the plane, but we were moving too quickly for me to pick out details. We taxied to the wharf, which, as usual, was partially under water at this time of year. The first little cabin I built was out of sight, but the third one, which had been my home for the last dozen years, looked in good shape. I couldn't see the satellite dish from where I was, but it turned out to have weathered the storms without problem.

Cabin Two, however, had lost its chimney. This had happened with monotonous regularity ever since I stopped wintering at Nuk Tessli and was not there to shovel snow off the roof. I had tried everything: built frames, attached chains, etc. The chimney was still there but lying on its side. It was an insulated unit, and too heavy for me to repair alone. I afforded another little smile to myself: it was no longer my responsibility.

The big damage was to an outhouse. It has always been difficult to dig a hole in the rocks around Nuk Tessli and I ended up with two shallow pits side by side. Rustic shelters and seats were built on top. If one got too gross I would put an "out of order" sign on it and have everyone use the other. A huge tree had leaned toward the outhouses for most of my tenure there. It was living, but a big crack had appeared in the trunk a few years before, and every time I looked at it, I wondered how long it would stay standing. Well, it was gone now; it had cleaved one of the outhouses in two. I cut out the branches that covered the trail to the usable structure, but the tree itself was rotten all through. It would be useless for firewood and would have to be dragged into the bush out of the way. Doron would have his own volunteers coming throughout the summer; that was another onerous job I could leave for them.

The only preparatory work I did was clean Cabin Three and Cabin One, and make sure there was a good supply of wood split for the stoves. A friend would be arriving in a few days; she would be leaving on the same plane that Doron would fly in with. For now, however, I had a small window of time to myself.

The Block

There is something special about the first hike of the year at Nuk Tessli. The trails are newly free of snow (for the most part) and littered with the windblown detritus of winter. Bits of bark, lichen and needles blend them with the forest floor. The trails will become dusty and worn all too soon, but now, in many places, they are hard to find and it is as if I am exploring the country all over again. A trail is good for covering ground quickly, but once it is made, you concentrate on finding the marks underfoot and no longer look where you are going.

June is spring in the high country. The deciduous bushes on the forest floor—mostly black huckleberry—are not yet leafed out, and the bare twigs smell of damp bark and lichen. The forest speaks of freshness, of a brave new world. An added bonus is that, usually, there are no biting insects at this time.

The first hike I always made was around "the block." The trail heads north from the cabins, picking a route through boulders (and, this time, another fallen tree), then enters the small meadow that does duty as a helicopter pad. At the nearer edge of the meadow was the spot where I had camped while building the first cabin. Big snowdrifts always lie here at the beginning of the season, and this year, courtesy of *nuk tessli*'s winter rampage, the sculpted piles were huge. They were rock-hard and steep-sided, and difficult to climb over.

The meadow had a few flatter snow patches on it, but most of it was covered in water. A lot was frozen, but not enough to support my weight. I always do the first hike of the year in gumboots. Farther back from the lake, taller sedges harboured the prolific white stars of the mountain marsh marigold. They are common everywhere, both below and above the treeline, and are in such a hurry to bloom, they will open under snow. On the outside, their buds exhibit an extraordinarily beautiful shade of ultramarine. The open flowers appear white to human eyes, but insects can see ultraviolet light and I don't doubt that there are unseen runes for pollinators on those seemingly colourless rays.

Beyond the meadow, more rocky forest is decorated with the odd snow patch. Soon the trail forks, and I took the branch that followed the creek up the mountain. The stream was roaring with runoff, brown and frothing, and audible long before I saw it. It is narrow and overhung with slide alder and willows; during flood times, the bare branches of the bushes are whipped back and forth by the current. I have called this Otter Creek, because these animals' tracks are present along it every winter. Otters are the original cross-country skiers. They make a big trough in the snow with their bodies. As they go up a slope, they leave footprints in the bottom of the trough. Downhill is just a big, happy skid. The tracks emerge from one hole in the ice, then disappear into another. These creatures mostly travel at night and I rarely saw them in winter, but have sometimes heard their whistles in summer and seen their heads pop up out of the water.

Otter Creek emerges from a small lake about a kilometre from the cabins. Halfway toward it is a little grassy area, always knee-deep in water when the runoff is high. I always meant to cut a trail out around the edge, but somehow every year I end up just picking a route; the water usually goes down fairly fast anyway. It was just above here that Bucky and Raffi chased the moose calf and drove it down the creek into the lake.

A little below Otter Lake is another fork in the trail. A single-log footbridge with a rope handrail crosses the creek at that point and from there the left branch heads up toward the Mammaries. Too much rotten snow would have made that hike a hard slog so early in the season, but I crossed the bridge to check on a patch of round-leaved violets, another very early bloomer. Sure enough, a few golden blossoms peeped out among the rocks. Even though it is fairly shady, the sun pokes under the trees and strikes this part of the creek bank so the snow goes early there. Like the mountain marsh marigolds, the violets bloom even before the pussy willows show their silvery buds.

I went back to my side of the creek and reached Otter Lake. Only part of it can be seen from this spot, a quiet inlet with a little ice still on it. Silvered, beetle-killed pines, remnants of the 1980s infestation, cluster on the far side like bearded patriarchs. The Lookout is visible, but most mountains are hidden. I often startle a pair of common mergansers or Barrow's goldeneyes there at this time of year. The current flowing out of the lake must bring food for small fishes and therefore be attractive to the birds. The striking black and white males of both species will soon be gone to their bachelor summer gatherings, but the females will breed in the area.

Back into the forest where yellow-rumped warblers were singing, after a few twists and turns, there emerged a pond. Still and dark at this time of year, it would soon be populated with bogbean and a floating organic sludge. I was hiking beside it with one prospective buyer when we discovered a large dragon-fly hatching from its larval skin. The bulbous-eyed husks these insects leave behind decorate the sedges everywhere in August.

I walked down a short trail through the rocky forest, this one flanked by white mountain rhododendron, not in flower yet, but dark green leaf spears were already poking out of lime-green buds. This is the misery bush of lower elevations that is such a nightmare to fight through, but at Nuk Tessli, it rarely exceeds waist height. In July it is laden with creamy trumpets, and it boasts lovely bronze and red leaves in the fall.

I reached another very wet open area, this one with three small ponds in it. They would host big yellow pond lilies and electric blue damsel flies later. Sometimes I have found long-toed salamanders here. The meadows were crowded with butterworts, but they wouldn't show their acid green leaves until the harder frosts abated. In one of the three little ponds was a free-floating relative called the bladderwort. Tiny traps attached to its floating roots are fringed with hairs. When the hairs encounter microscopic organisms, the trap opens in one five-thousandth of a second, sucking both water and the organism inside. The hairs close and prevent escape. It is a real horror-movie plant, swimming freely around and gobbling up its prey. Good job it is so small.

None of these were visible now, not even the early-blooming yellow anemone. I slogged through boot-high water and brown, matted sedges, then into a stretch of forest again. I was now heading back to the cabins. Three more trees were down along this section. I dreaded to think how much clearing would have to be done on the trails, but as I travelled around later, it became evident that the worst wind had been funnelled into a very narrow band. The cabins had been directly in its path. I imagined the wind coming down the frozen lake and smashing into the buildings, gust after gust, before wreaking its trail of destruction into the forest. Had I been there, I would have been terrified.

. . . .

Doreen, like so many friends I now have, was originally a client at Nuk Tessli. She had been part of a group that had come in late July after the big snow year of 2007. Normally we would have had a good show of flowers in the alpine by then, but every time we tried to climb high, we were turned back by creeks we couldn't cross or ended up wading through deep snow. It made for some spectacular scenery; fortunately, most of the clients in that group were interested in the hiking rather than the flowers. Doreen,

Badger and Harry swimming.

however, is a plant enthusiast as well as a photographer, and was pleased that she could squeeze in a final hike at Nuk Tessli while I was still going to be there. It was a little early to expect much to be blooming, but a plant enthusiast can get excited over the tiniest little bud, and a photographer doesn't even need flowers.

We headed for the Mammaries. Although it was only a few days after the hike around the block, the snow was melting fast and the high country would now be a little easier to manage. The weather was dull, and large patches of ground were under water or snow. As we splashed up the wet meadows to the edge of the treeline, fox sparrows and gold-crowned sparrows sang. Both are special birds for me at Nuk Tessli. The gold-crowned sparrow sings in the subalpine only, and his four poignant clear notes are the sound I most associate with that beautiful moment when the land sheds the forest and the open world is spread below. Sparrows of all kinds have very variable songs and I have

On the way to North Pass Lake.

listened to tapes of gold-crowned sparrows that bear absolutely no resemblance to the birds' songs in my area.

We encountered a lot of snow below the treeline, but the south-facing slope of the Mammaries gets blasted by sun and wind all winter and is naked long before the surrounding country. We sank knee-deep on the plateau (where the stone circle was still completely buried) and it was not until we reached the bare slopes that we finally found our reward. Clumps of red-flowered roseroot, various draba species, and a few early heathers. Sky-blue Jacob's ladders clung to little sheltered pockets among the wind-beaten rocks and tundra. It is particularly hard to photograph as the flower is on a slender stalk and thrashes about in the wind.

A couple of days later, we headed toward what I call North Pass Lake. The trapping family used to travel that way to get into the next valley. Their trail was so boggy and overgrown I was never able to follow it for long. I had figured out another route up Beach Creek, which flows into my lake about one and a half kilometres from the cabins. The year I broke my leg, Dylan and the volunteers started to brush out a trail; this now makes an easy way to access the North Pass.

We canoed early to the trail head; the dogs, who are very familiar with this routine, swam and ran around the shore.

The trail is deeply sheltered, and it is very pretty walking up beside this creek. The yellow round-leaved violets were abundant—the best display I have ever seen. Both Doreen and I found it hard to pass a single clump without trying to take its picture; our climb was therefore very slow. We finally reached more open country. Very little vegetation was poking though the winter-rotted mat of sedges, and snowmelt was pouring down the meadows in roaring waterfalls. In these conditions, densely packed clumps of a miniscule, vivid orange mushroom can be found. I haven't been able to identify the species. It grows only on mouse bathrooms. Small rodents build a whole network of chambers and tunnels underneath the snow for their winter homes. They make round nests of grass to sleep in, and always use a separate spot for a bathroom. Their little poops form a mass the size of a couple of grapefruits. It is on these that the bright orange mouse-poop fungus grows. As spring advances and the meadows dry up, the organism disappears.

The trail stays just below the treeline. It is a bit more shady than the route to the Mammaries, and the snow lies later. Soon there was no bare ground visible at all.

One or two lakes partially open gave us wonderful ice colours and reflections of the panorama of mountains behind them, but we stopped short of the North Pass Lake. We could see it from a height of land, but it wasn't worth the effort of getting there. Pools of meltwater spangled its surface, but it was still frozen solid.

Life With Doron

Doron is an easy man to like. He is full of enthusiasm about life, and he can laugh at his mistakes. As well as the lumber and a new chainsaw, a variety of unidentifiable packages were unloaded from the plane he flew in on. Doron refused my help to carry these things; in truth my offer had been only half-hearted, as rough walking without sticks was quite painful for me. He happily made himself at home in Cabin One. He would move to Cabin Two after his helpers had arrived and the chimney had been replaced.

The following morning, I heard an odd noise coming from the wharf: a rhythmic sucking sound. I couldn't see what was happening from my cabin so went to investigate. One of the objects Doron had brought was a heavy bundle of folded blue plastic. It was now revealed to be a large inflatable canoe. Doron had used it in Alaska to transport tourists on the guiding trip he had made before he came to Nuk Tessli. The canoe came complete with an outboard motor. The only boat motor that had been on the lake in my twenty-three years here had been brought in for a fish survey. I had ridden along with the two technicians in their rubber raft while they measured the depth of the lake (sixty metres at the deepest part) and set nets for twenty-minute periods at various points to see what was swimming around in there. I had never wanted an outboard motor. I am no mechanic and if the thing went wrong it

Doron paddling.

would be expensive to fly out and fix. I was content to live my life at paddle-speed and to bow to the vagaries of the wind.

The sucking noise came from a foot pump that Doron was using to inflate the canoe. He had found my paddle store, and a couple of these lay upon the wharf. The motor was a loaner from the float plane company; Doron's own would be coming later. He fitted it on the frame that had been inserted at the back of the canoe and asked me aboard for a ride. I hate sitting in front. I feel precarious and out of control. I grabbed a paddle and gingerly lowered myself aboard, but it felt quite stable. Doron fired the motor and we slowly chugged into the middle of the lake and steered toward the mountains. It felt weird to be moving along with no physical effort.

In the middle of the lake, the motor coughed and died. Doron pulled at the starter cord a couple of times. The motor fired up, chugged a few seconds, then died again. Oh well, we were now in a situation that I was familiar with. But as I lifted my paddle,

Yoga pose on the North Ridge. Photo by Crystal Watson.

Doron took it from my grasp. Apparently the second paddle still lay on the wharf. Had *nuk tessli* been blowing, we could have made a sail with a coat and drifted most of the way home, but the lake was uncharacteristically calm. The sky was soft and grey; the water had a silvery cast. It was undeniably pleasant to move quietly through this silvery stillness, but it felt odd to be given the role of a sack of potatoes. Usually I was the person who made the decisions and who did the brunt of the work. This change in status was welcome in some ways, but it was going to take some getting used to.

The outboard motor was the first of many innovations Doron brought to Nuk Tessli. The second, and the one that impressed me most, was a router to set up wireless for the Internet. Had I known how cheap it was and easy to install, I would have bought it years ago. Satellite Internet had arrived at Nuk Tessli in 2004; my computer was plugged directly into the modem. Adding Wi-Fi meant that Doron could call out with an iPhone. I had never bothered to investigate such technology as I had no idea it would work here. Many wwoofers brought laptops and phones but they all had to use my computer for emails. Even these young people had not told me of the possibilities of these toys.

Unfortunately the modems had to stay where they were in Cabin Three as there was no spare cable, and the signal didn't stretch very far beyond the walls. Later, when the place was full of Israelis, every morning would see them gathered on my deck all texting, phoning or using their laptops to contact friends back home. I thought this quite amazing: the world had passed me by. I had become bushed.

The third innovation was a hot tub! Doron brought something called a Snorkel Stove: a sheet metal heater that could be submerged in water. Companies sold expensive wooden containers to complete the tub, but Doron planned to make a simple one from standard lumber lined with a heavy-duty tarp. He decided to put it on the point beyond the rock pile that protected Nuk Tessli from the worst of the winds. Out came the chainsaw and down came three or four trees. When I built my very first cabin at Lonesome Lake, I logged just to get space, and was appalled at the terrible mess I had created. The scars never disappeared. At Nuk Tessli I logged for safety but was very careful to leave certain trees to artistically complement the view. As a result, the marks of destruction had quickly grown over, and the whole place soon looked wild again. I winced a bit as the new trees went down, but at least I wouldn't be responsible for the cleanup.

After a few days, another Beaver came in loaded with supplies, and it also brought a man in his late twenties. Like most of the young Israelis who would eventually come over, Amotz had recently finished his stint in the army; unlike the others, Amotz had no designs on going to university. He was a happy individual who could turn his hand to most things. He loved life and was passionate about the beauties of his country. His parents had a boutique B & B, which he had helped to build, beside the Sea of Galilee. He showed me pictures on the computer.

Amotz and Doron completed most of the hot tub. They also ripped the steps out of the porch in Cabin Two and prepared to insulate it and install a compost toilet. After being queen of Nuk Tessli for twenty-three years, I would finally have a throne! But in truth I preferred going to the outhouse. There was no door and I had a nice view of trees there. In spring, I could watch the birds. Sometimes, when the place was very busy, it was the only spot that would give me a few minutes' peace and quiet.

The first of the clients whom I had booked arrived: two couples from Prince George and a woman from Ontario. I tried to get them all on the same plane, as a Beaver can hold six passengers, but there was apparently a problem as one of the men weighed 140 kilograms. Doron and I were wondering whether he would be able to get himself over the rocky trail to the outhouse (the compost toilet wasn't installed at that point). When the plane taxied in, the float on the passenger side was underwater. But the man bounced down out of the plane (sinking the floating part of the wharf with a big whoosh) and ran around the mountains much better than I could. His wife was probably not that small but she seemed diminutive beside him. When they took a canoe out, there was so much difference in the weight from one end to the other that the prow was clear of the water and the woman perched up there like a carved figurehead.

Clients in the hot tub.

The lady from Ontario was fun. She dressed well and looked quite elegant, so it was a surprise to see her flinging herself into any situation with gusto. She was the wife of a pig farmer and later sent me pictures of herself clutching half-grown porkers. She was quite the yoga expert.

She liked standing on her head. Apparently she blew the candles out on her last birthday cake from that position. Once again, this is someone who came as a client, but I have continued to stay in touch with her. I might not consider myself a people person, but I have made a lot of friends at Nuk Tessli.

Oren arrived from Israel, and later his girlfriend Inbal did too. Most Israeli names have meanings. Inbal is the clapper of a bell, Oren is a pine tree, Sela means rock and Doron translates as a gift. All of these newcomers were fresh from the army: that's the way it is in Israel. Kids leave school and go straight into the forces, men for three years, women for two. Many then stay on for a

Inbal baking challah in the stone oven.

while as then they get paid to teach recruits. They are therefore in their late twenties when they go to university.

Before I came to Canada I had travelled the world widely, visiting thirty-four countries and living in six of them. As I have no proclivity for organized religion, Israel had never particularly interested me as a destination. I now found it to be a fascinating place. I had thought it was all desert but the climate is varied: the northwest is humid and only the south and east are dry. The desert, however, is dotted with farming communities growing produce that is shipped around the world. Even dairy farms operate in the desert. All food, including fodder for the cows, is grown hydroponically. At Nuk Tessli I had an endless supply of fabulous water right outside the door. How on earth could hydroponic farms happen in Israel's deserts? Apparently a series of deep, ancient cisterns, already well established in biblical times, stay full for about nine months of the year and contain enough water to grow crops. Israel is also a major bird flyway. Migratory species that travel from Europe to Africa do not want to cross the Mediterranean, so they squeeze by over Israel. Needless to say, should I ever wish to travel there in the future, I will have many places to stay.

During the day, we all fed ourselves. (I would not have wanted to eat my breakfast halfway through the morning!) But we each cooked part of the evening meal on our own stoves, then met together in my cabin to eat it. It was the only place with enough room for everyone to sit down. It is a good job that I am comfortable with being on the fringe of a group as sometimes I was the only person at the table who was not speaking Hebrew.

I did some of the guiding, but because of my bad knee I couldn't manage the longer hikes. I couldn't go out on consecutive days either. When Doron took clients, they all spoke highly of him. Despite his Everest credentials, he went slowly and considerately. He wouldn't have been able to show them my pet trees—the lightning-struck one, the hollow column with regularly spaced woodpecker holes that looks like a flute, the burned-out hull of the monster tree that makes a sonorous drum sound when beaten—but he did try to learn some of the more obvious flowers.

The Gift

I would be leaving Nuk Tessli at the end of the first week in August and wanted to get to the North Ridge and the Mammary Meadows one last time. The calendar-picture flower displays would be at their peak. Because long hiking days were becoming so painful, the best way for me to enjoy the meadows would be to camp just below the treeline. I have always kept dogs as pack animals. They carry my gear on longer hikes. Even allowing for the fact that their food has to be brought along, it still makes life easier for me. A healthy dog can pack ten kilograms on a normal day. They generally carried heavier loads than I did.

Normally, when I backpacked with these two dogs, I kept Harry on a lead. On his own, Badger would never go very far. If both animals were loose and they saw a caribou or a rabbit, they would likely be gone with all my food, tents and cookware. Even if they returned, their packs or the contents could be damaged or lost. However, I was now using two poles to hike with and couldn't take a leashed dog at the same time.

Doron had friends staying, and they and his work crew decided to take a day off. They figured they might as well head in the direction I wanted to go. Because they would be more or less empty-handed, they would carry my camp up for me. This was a wonderful gift.

There is a lovely spot at the top of Long Meadow, just below the treeline. A flat, dry space just big enough for a single tent is tucked in behind a large clump of short, dense subalpine fir that would provide plenty of dead twigs for firewood. A tiny, mountain-fresh stream trickles close by.

As usual, I was up and away long before anyone else and reached the campsite in time to bask in the morning sun and wait. Soon the hikers appeared, trudging up Long Meadow toward me. I could see why Doron covered the ground so easily. He would step and rest, step and rest, but the pace was effortless. His hiking boots were still among freight that had not yet caught up with him, and he was wearing gumboots, which didn't seem to faze him at all. No doubt on his own he would have travelled faster, but although his friends behind were looking red-faced and somewhat more dishevelled, they were easily keeping up so the pace must have suited them as well. They dropped my gear and continued on their way.

In alpine country, there are no trees tall enough to hang food out of reach of bears. I simply cook and store supplies well away from the tent; I have never had any trouble. I hopped across the little stream to a stony rise where I levered a few rocks out of the way and built a small fire. When I had done with it, I would replace the rocks and there would be no sign of my ever having been there. From the rise I had a view down the way I had come to the long sprawl of my lake far below, with its by now very familiar panorama of mountains behind.

That afternoon, I stuck fairly close to camp, exploring every niche and nook and cranny that I knew from past experience might harbour flowers. I was not expecting anything revolutionary, but light is everything in a composition, and I was looking for that perfect picture to take away with me. I had started my wilderness career with a film camera; always mindful of cost, I had rationed my photos carefully. What great fun it had been to go digital.

View toward Nuk Tessli from the North Ridge.

The weather was not the best, but it wasn't raining. The flowers, however, more than made up for it. After two poor seasons and a late winter, the displays this year were spectacular. *Putting on their best dresses*, as Janis would have said. Red paintbrush, blue lupin, yellow senecio, white valerian and white bog orchids, which flood the air with a scent like freesias, abounded everywhere. Orchids have good years and bad years. When one orchid species is doing well it seems that all of them follow suit.

The following day I hiked the whole of the North Ridge, just like I used to on a day trip when I first came to Nuk Tessli.

The rock alpines on the exposed slopes were finished, but in the lee of the ridge they were in their prime—mountain goldenrod, sedums, potentillas and that precious gem, the incomparable deep blue alpine harebell. Its two-centimetre trumpets are open to the sky and borne on tiny, thin stems. The blossoms may be as big as the whole of the rest of the plant put together. They tolerate the harshest of stony environments where nothing else will grow, so their fragility is even more precious.

It was dull and cloudy; the wind blew and tossed the blossoms every which way, and sometimes a few spits of rain rattled on my parka hood. I was in seventh heaven.

Alpine harebell.

As I headed down toward camp, I steered a course for the stone circle. I paused for a moment in its centre. All around were the peaks, ridges, creeks and hollows of my Queendom. I remembered picking routes up this gully or that ridge and standing on various peaks. I remembered the caribou dissolving one by one into a blizzard, and the high yap of wolf cubs floating toward me on the wind. And I remembered the shy hidden alpines and the vast nodding carpets of flowers. What a life I have had up here.

That evening, the clouds parted a little and I was treated to a pretty sunset, but the real bonus came the following morning. A bit of cloud hung about, but the sky was clear over the North Ridge where the sun would rise. Monarch Mountain and all the big peaks seen at the head of Nuk Tessli were hidden from the camp by a rocky mound and I climbed up there before the first rays hit the summits. All the valleys spread below me were clogged with a grey fog, the dark peaks rising out of them like islands. Where I stood, the air was crystal clear. A pink glow hit the top of Monarch Mountain. The colour intensified and changed from pink to orange to yellow as the shadow moved slowly down the mountain. Soon the sun climbed over the North Ridge and its long-fingered golden glow lit the sedums and yarrow growing in the rock cracks beside my feet. The valleys were still drowned in their fuzzy-edged sea. Truly I was in the lap of the gods.

The north side of the rocky knoll had a sun-cupped snow slab. It was frozen, so very slippery, and I worked my way down it carefully and slowly picked a route back to camp. Paintbrushes make wonderful photography subjects when they are backlit. The colourful bracts filter the light like stained glass, and the hairy rims give the plant a silver halo.

Midmorning, I packed up the camp and started down. The most reliable dog, Badger, carried his pack, but Harry's was folded up and shoved into Badger's so I wouldn't have to bother with a lead.

Halfway back to Nuk Tessli there is a pretty spot where a creek runs into a pool at the top of a small meadow. I generally stop there with hikers and encourage them to drink from the icy stream. Many parts of the world have a little saying that if you drink their water you will always return. I have often told that story at this place. I sat on my favourite rock beside the creek, scooped a cup into it and made a ritual toast to all the times I had received such pleasure at this spot. I could always come again, of course; I did not live too far away. In fact Doron would like me to do some future guiding. It is an attractive proposition. All I would have to do is putter around with people and look at flowers. I wouldn't have to organize flights, pay the bills or cook. But first I'll have to get a new knee—and who knows what else the future might bring.

....

I had one last duty before I left Nuk Tessli. It was to host a bus tour. They had been coming to Nuk Tessli for seventeen years. The participants travel by road to Nimpo on an eight-day round trip that includes the ferry from Bella Coola to Vancouver Island. They stay two nights at Nimpo Lake, and up to forty people may arrive at Nuk Tessli during the day. They are divided into three groups and each group needs two or three planes to fly them around. Tweedsmuir Air manages the logistics of this like clockwork.

Badger packing.

Most of the visitors are seniors, many in their eighties and some in their nineties. I think they are very brave; for some, the pilot has to place their feet on the ladder as they lower themselves to the dock. Getting back into the plane, many need a somewhat inelegant boost. Will this be me in the future? But they laugh at their difficulties and it doesn't stop them from enjoying themselves.

The worst fear for me was that they would hurt themselves falling among the rocks. A few did, but fortunately none received serious damage, and the worst falls were always when a tour guide was present. (As there is only one tour guide and one bus driver, one of the three groups is unescorted.) The float, where the visitors first tread after they get out of the plane, is a bit bouncy and I always hold them until they have their hand on the rail beside the steps that will lead them up to the firm dock.

I well remember one lady whose balance was uncertain. She managed the wobbly float with no problem but then fell over on the solid dock. She insisted it had moved. I couldn't lift her alone and had to ask for help from a fellow tourist. Another lady I also remember well. We got her onto the deck in front of Cabin Two but she was not agile enough to walk farther. She smoked like a chimney so I gave her an empty sardine can as an ashtray and prepared to take everyone else for a little hike around the property. I would show them the cabins and tell them a bit of the history of the place. The lady didn't mind being on her own; she was a cheerful soul. After we had seated her she asked, "Are we going home by boat?" I explained that no boat could get here! The plane would come in a couple of hours and take them on a flightseeing tour. When the rest of her group arrived back from their hike she said, "When's the boat coming?" Oh well, I guess she couldn't walk well enough to get lost.

On the whole, however, the bus tour clients have a great time, and they are a lot of fun. Many of them have very interesting stories to tell. I give them tea and my famous stone-oven-baked bread. They leave me their lunches—bananas, roast beef sand-wiches and cookies, all stuff I often don't have at Nuk Tessli, so real treats.

The last bus tour plane disappeared over the ridge toward Nimpo; I now had no more obligations to Nuk Tessli. I was offi-cially retired. By pure chance, that day also marked my sixty-fifth birthday. Friends arrived on the empty planes that came to pick up the tourists, and we would have one last party.

Doron had been away for a few days and his group came back as well so the place became very crowded indeed. I had originally wondered if I was going to have to sleep in a tent during the sum-mer, but Doron always insisted that I should have Cabin Three to myself. This was very generous, as the other two buildings were bursting at the seams. That night, seventeen people were jammed around the tables. Doron's wife, Suzan, had flown in a few days before. I had made a little cardboard key and wrote on it, "The Key to Nuk Tessli." I stifled my feelings and made a little speech, then handed it over to Doron.

I have known other people who sold properties they had lov-ingly developed to new owners with whom they had little in com-mon. They were instantly alienated from their lifetime's work. I am fortunate that Doron and his family will cherish Nuk Tessli in the same way that I did. I will remain friends with Doron and never lose my connection with these mountains.

I had been shipping out my possessions every time there had been plane space. The pilots had been storing it in Tweedsmuir Air's hangar. There was a lot of stuff, because for many years I had no other home, and everything had been stored in the mountains. The artwork had been left on the walls until last: my friends helped me pack it. The walls I had covered, narrow board by narrow board, in the millennium year looked bereft when they were stripped. My friends took a separate plane as I, the dogs and my gear would fill a Beaver. One came in to pick me up the following morning. It was another beautiful day. I

The keys to Nuk Tessli. Photo by Paul vanPeenen.

had so far handled the whole situation in what I imagined had
been a calm and logical manner, but when I climbed into the
Beaver, I was unable to say goodbye.

The plane lifted off toward the mountains as it had done so
many times before. No smoke on this occasion, just the clean
rock and shining snow rising into the heavenly blue. We curved
toward the Chilcotin, bumping slightly, and I took a last fuzzy
picture of the cabins on their point jutting into the lake. We wob-
bled over the sharp ridge at the foot of Nuk Tessli and followed
the river valley between the smaller peaks to the flat lands of the
interior plateau.

At Nimpo, the pilot and dock boy took my boxes out of
the plane and stacked them onto the wharf before disappearing
into their busy day. I went to the office to pick up my keys, then
fetched the van from its storage place behind the woodpile at

the back of the resort. I loaded the dogs and what I could carry. I would have to make a second trip to fetch the rest of my stuff.

After I had been in the bush for several weeks, the vehicle seemed awkward and alien to me. It smelled of old oil, metal, synthetic materials and dust. I climbed into the driver's seat and switched on the motor. I drove away from the float plane base and into my new life. I did not look back at the mountains.

Acknowledgements

T hank you Trudy and Jack Turner, who gave me the oppor-
tunity to start, and Elizabeth and Alan Bell, Katie Hayhurst
and Dennis Kuch, and Corry Lunn, who have generously
supported my wilderness habit all these years. Thank you to all
the many volunteers who helped me keep Nuk Tessli going for so
long, particularly Nick Berwian, without whom the third cabin
would not have been built. Thanks also to the anonymous young
man with the long hair, beard and cobbled-together jeans, who
opened the second door.

Chris Czajkowski was born and raised in England, where she studied agriculture. As a young adult, in 1971, she started to backpack around the world. She lived and travelled in the southern hemisphere for nearly eight years and arrived in British Columbia, Canada, at the end of 1979. Her first jobs were on dairy farms but the eastern Okanagan was too crowded for her and she soon found her way to the West Chilcotin, where she realized her dream of living in the wilderness.

The first cabin she built was near Lonesome Lake, forty kilometres from the nearest road, about 450 kilometres north of Vancouver. Four years later she travelled higher into the mountains and, working completely alone in country too rugged for a wheelbarrow, built another cabin on a remote unnamed lake close to the southern tip of Tweedsmuir Provincial Park. Two more buildings followed; these became the nucleus of a small, high-altitude resort, The Nuk Tessli Alpine Experience. Access was by two-day hike through largely trackless mountains, or a flight in a small bush plane. She lived at Nuk Tessli for twenty-three years.

Chris started writing in the mid-1980s by sending letters describing her time at Lonesome Lake to Peter Gzowski's *Morningside* on CBC Radio. She has since published eleven books about her wilderness life.

www.wildernessdweller.ca